CYBERSECURITY

A Comprehensive Beginner's Guide to learn the Realms of Cybersecurity from A-Z

ELIJAH LEWIS

TABLE OF CONTENTS

Introduction

Cybersecurity has been developing as a new concept in the world. It has the potential to disrupt world peace and also to maintain it all the more better. I had been an avid reader of science fiction for the past few years. One day I was reading a novel about a cyberattack on the state's nuclear facility when I snoozed for a while and had a nightmare. What I saw in the dream resembled the climax of one of the movies from the X-Men franchise in which Apocalypse triggers the nuclear missiles around the globe to kick off and hit the targets in other countries. I saw that a powerful hacking group that belonged to a rogue nation-state hacked into the computer network systems of North Korea and released the nuclear warheads aiming at the United States. This kicked off a series of attacks and rebuttals from other nations. It was just like a chain reaction that went on end until there was nothing left in the world. Only the thought of it was destructive, to say the least.

More than once, I think that what would have happened had North Korea succeeded in shutting down the power grid of the United States instead of stealing documents from Sony Pictures Entertainment. What would have happened? What would be the reaction of the United States had it happened? Some defense analysts believe cybersecurity attacks are a blessing in disguise as they offer countries to use proxies to vindicate the feelings of revenge. It saves the world from landing into an all-out war. Some say that it is the most serious threat in the history of the world as the attacker is unknown which causes confusion, and confusion will result in a state of war. So, this can make the matter worse.

What This Book Has to Offer

This book aims at covering a wide range of topics related to cybersecurity issues. This book is written for the students of technology and international relations, as it discussed from a wide range of aspects the issue of cybersecurity and its geopolitical repercussions. This book is divided into different chapters that deal with a wide range of topics and subtopics. Here is a chapter-wise breakdown of the book to give you an insight into what you will find inside the chapters.

- The first chapter aims at dealing with the fundamentals of cybersecurity. You will have the definition of cybersecurity. You will learn about the importance of the protection of smartphones and web applications, and social media and its role in cybersecurity. The next topic is the importance of email networks and certain electronic devices and their role in ensuring security. The chapter goes on to deal with the issue of the emergence of cybersecurity in the modern world. I'll discuss in detail how cybersecurity as a field of study rose to prominence after hackers broke into several facilities and state institutions. The chapter concludes by explaining what dark web is and why it is so important to hackers. It explains what happens on the dark web, how it operates, and how a common person can use it. I'll also debunk the myth and prove that dark web is, after all, not so much dark. Instead, common users use dark web to ensure their online privacy. However, some arguments go directly against the dark web especially the tendency of the dark web to facilitate some illegal activities such as transportation of some banned drugs right through postal services.

- The second chapter explains the why a cybercriminal attacks a facility why it infiltrates a critical infrastructure. I'll explain the importance of the motive of profit behind an attack. Cyber-espionage is one motive that keeps hackers on edge. I have categorized espionage into two parts, such as driven by the corporate sector and backed by the state machinery. A corporate sector spies on its competitors to steal their trade secrets while the state machinery does this to know the strategic state of its competitors. Then I'll move on to explain what type of industries are at the weak end of the spectrum when it comes to a cyberattack. I'll explain what the point of attraction that a hacker sees when he attacks an industry is. I'll cover up different industries such as the health sector, the public sector departments, the financial firms and the food sector.

- Cyberattacks are not always about a few computers and the internet of things (IoT). Sometimes things go into the physical world and that's what we dub as social engineering. I'll go into the depths of social engineering such as how to execute it and what are the objectives of social engineering. I'll explain how to conduct a social engineering attack efficiently. I'll also explain why social engineering attack becomes necessary to accomplish a hacker's objective. Several factors come into play when hacker plans a social engineering attack. This spans around the trust factor between the manipulator and the victim. Social engineering is a cunning method to manipulate an employee of the organization that a hacker wants to attack. At the end of the chapter, I have given some practical steps to counter this kind of manipulation and attack. If you give it a careful read, you will be able to train your employees to conquer such a situation effectively. I'll explain why the employees of an organization are the most powerful tool and at the same time, are also the most vulnerable part of an organization.

- The fourth chapter goes on to explain what cyber terrorism is. I'll explain the basic definitions of a cyberattack, and then I will move on to explaining different types of cyber terrorism that are prevalent in the world nowadays. The chapter carries a detailed discussion on the effects of cyber terrorism on the world and also how it affects the security scenario of the world. The chapter ends up on multiple countermeasures in the wake of cyber terrorism. I intend to equip you with the latest knowledge about different types of cyber terrorism and how you can counter it. From this angle, I'll explain the importance of cybersecurity in the modern world.

- The next chapter explains what cyber-espionage is. You will be navigated through different tactics that cyber-spies use to penetrate a computer system. I'll give a thorough look at the current cyber-espionage affairs. The chapter will end on explaining some latest cyber-espionage attacks that have seriously affected different facilities across the world.

- The sixth chapter of the book is quite an interesting one, and it is pretty panoramic in its scope. Cyberwarfare is pretty common nowadays and it has become a tool to start a proxy war in place of going to an all-out war to minimize the threats. In the start of the chapter, I'll give a brief history of cyberwarfare. Then I will move on to have an overview of the weapons that are used in a cyberwarfare attack. You will find a list of weapons along with a brief explanation of each of them. Then I'll move on to discuss about the defensive measures that a nation-state can take against cyberwarfare.

- The seventh chapter revolves around ethical hacking and why it is so important to ensure cybersecurity. I'll explain what the dangers are that can plague a cyber system. I will explain who an ethical hacker is what important job he has to secure the cyberspace of an organization. You will get to know the timing of the ethical hacking attack, like how to stage an attack and what are the objectives that you can achieve through an ethical hacking attack. My argument is to convince you of the importance of ethical hacking and how it can contribute to the security of your organization.

- The next chapter focuses on the internet of things and the vulnerabilities they can carry with them. I'll explain why it is important to check the internet of things before you buy them and what are the inherent weakness that plague the internet of thing devices. The chapter is important because of the fact that we ignore how vulnerable our mobile phone and tablet are. I'll discuss in detail the types of weaknesses in these devices, and then I'll proceed toward the remedial measures to overcome these vulnerabilities. The top-level vulnerability is without a doubt buying a device that doesn't have these kind of weaknesses.

- The next chapter deals with the vulnerabilities in the critical infrastructure in a country. I'll explain what these vulnerabilities are and how you can overcome them. One important thing to keep in mind is that what can be the possible repercussions if we don't pay heed to the strength of the critical infrastructure. I'll explain what the trickledown effect is and how a single deadly attack on a key critical infrastructure can result in creating chaos in the entire system. How the public will start panicking and how the enemy will win a war without fighting. The chapter, like others, ends on suggesting some key steps to safeguard the critical infrastructure.

- The next chapter is a brief one but a very important one. It deals with the economic cost of a cybersecurity attack and a cybersecurity strategy. It encompasses the cost of an ethical hacking test, the cost of countermeasures such as hiring experts, and buying some precious antivirus programs.

- The second last chapter of the book carries solutions to the problems of cybersecurity. I'll discuss in detail which solutions are viable to domestic users and the enterprise users. I have categorized these issues into two sets; one deals with the prevention of the cyberattacks right at the source while the other deals with the issues that arise after you have been attacked. One example of such a remedy is antivirus software that detects the malware and deletes it from your system.

- The last chapter of the book is very comprehensive as it deals with the current and future trends of cybersecurity. I will explain the current trends that hackers and defenders are using across the world. Then I will explain what the future trends in cybersecurity are and how the industry will shape up with the increasing awareness in the field and a rise in cyberattacks.

This book is for anyone who has an interest in cybersecurity. The reader can be a student of technology, a businessman, and a head of a public department. In whatever position you are, you will find the book extremely useful. I have explored each subtopic in great depth to sensitize the readers about cybersecurity and how it is going to affect the international relations and certain geopolitical situations across the world. You don't need to have any kind of prior knowledge of cybersecurity. You should just need to have a working knowledge of computers and the internet.

Chapter 1

Fundamentals of Cybersecurity

Each day sees a new cutting edge innovation in the world of information technology, and it is being embraced with open arms due to its ease-of-use and efficiency. The way technology is making progress; its value for people across the world will see a tremendous increase. With the dawn of each day, a wide range of businesses and corporations are securing their space in the cyber world. Businesses are embracing e-commerce, online payment systems and social networking to boost up their revenues. No one can deny the benefits that businesses have attained through entering the cyber world but this world is not so safe after all. It is the amount of anonymity it offers to users that have become an apple of discord for big businesses and individual users. The cyber-world harbors a huge number of cybercriminals that make cyberspace a little bit creepy and mysterious.

If you are running an online business that also involves frequent transactions of funds, you should understand how cybersecurity works and how you can form a shield to protect yourself against heinous designs of cybercriminals. To start with, you should have an in-depth knowledge of what cybersecurity is and how it works. The concept of cybersecurity is as old as the cyberspace itself is, but it came to limelight only after the world learned about the existence of viruses in the cyberspace. A number of words namely spyware, worms, malware, Trojan-horse, and worms, found their place in information technology (IT) vocabulary around forty years ago.

In the 1970s, Robert Thomas, who had been a researcher at BBN Technologies in Massachusetts, made progress in creating the first computer worm named The Creeper. It was a kind of virus that had the power to infect computers one after another. Each computer it hopped on and infected, it left a specific message titled as 'I'M THE CREEPER: CATCH ME IF YOU CAN.' The creation of a virus created the need for an antivirus named as The Reaper. The Reaper had a special job to chase Creeper and remove it from computers.

Robert Morris conceived the idea of measuring the dimensions of the internet, and for this purpose, he created a program that invaded Unix terminals. The worm was so lethal and aggressive that it slowed down the speed of computers up to the extent that they became unusable. Robert was put on trial under Computer Fraud and Abuse Act and afterward convicted. Since then, viruses became deadlier and harder to control. This incident kicked off the start of cybersecurity.

What Is Cybersecurity?

Cybersecurity is defined as a set of technologies, practices and processes that are created and designed to safeguard programs, network systems that connect computers, software and virtual data against any invasion or an attempt to damage. Criminals are always after the data that is stored on your computer system and that's why they sneak into computer systems and steal your precious information. They use network systems and servers to access the data. Cybersecurity slashes the risk of cyberattacks and protects individuals and organizations from any kind of unauthorized exploitation of network systems and technologies.

Cybersecurity involves people, technology and processes while it is in the implementation phase. Each term has its own role in setting up proper safety. This three-pronged strategy is meant to aid organizations from sophisticated and organized cyberattacks in addition to protecting them from any kind of common low-profile internal threats. The intensity of these attacks depends on the innovation and invention capacity of the attacker.

With the passage of time, the volume of threats is on the rise, and their evolution is significant especially when security companies are leaving no stone unturned to defend computer systems across the world from a different type of cyberattacks. Cyberattacks can be lethal and expensive for businesses. In the first place, corporations and businesses have to suffer financial loss in the form of damaged network systems that need immediate reparation. The second most common damage that businesses have to endure is in the form of data breach. Even if the lost data is recovered right after the cyberattack, the damage that is inflicted on the reputation of the business is beyond any calculation. Cyberattacks are getting more destructive as new techniques and methods have been evolving fast.

With the advances in the sophistication of technology, cybersecurity has turned into an inseparable part of online businesses. The corporate sector is not increasing its focus on the development of viable responses that will cut down the damage of a cyberattack. In view, these rising numbers of threats and viruses, it is crucial that we better understand the vulnerabilities that are attached to the cyber landscape. Certain risk assessment and management processes need to be established to identify the best security measures that must be adopted by the business sector. A comprehensive cybersecurity strategy should be developed in consultation with legal brains and insurance agencies for creating a sound and foolproof defensive strategy that could provide a shield against short-term and long-term safety of assets.

Protection of Smartphones and Web Devices

The tremendous growth of cellphones and tablets has created a vulnerable landscape in the cyber world. First of all, the number of mobile devices is pretty large, nearly countless. In addition, there is either an absence of any meaningful security mechanism on the devices and if there is one in place, it is being marginalized because of weaknesses in the system. Malware is inching towards its full development and is being used in combination with botnet attacks. Mobile attacks are becoming a hot target for cybercriminals. If you are running a financial consultancy firm, you have to welcome a number of guests each at your office, and more guests mean that you will have to permit an equal number of mobile devices to penetrate your networks. This increases the vulnerability factor in your corporation.

Smartphones, pads, tablets, and laptops usually remain connected to the internet all the time; therefore, they need to be protected from an anticipated attack with the help of state-of-the-science protection solutions for your device. There have been plenty of innovations that can elevate the quality of security of your device and against such devices if the attacker is using a mobile device to stage an attack. Innovations have ensured the availability of high-end safety mechanisms that were only available to large networks. Individuals and small firms can access them and make use of mobile phones and any their device perfectly safe to use. A device protection system must include a remote management system for effective security. The point is to eliminate the user-input factor from the security realm to minimize vulnerability.

As an owner of a finance consultancy firm, you should ensure that your staff has secured mobile devices. Request them to install real-time anti-virus software, and application protection is also essential to ensure cybersecurity. Another important part of cybersecurity is password management application. By nature, we go for ease of use when it comes to setting passwords. We cannot just remember them because there are just so many of them such as separate passwords of email accounts, social media networks, online workspace apps, banking apps and many other different virtual spaces. When we find it difficult to remember, we either set a single password to all the applications and websites or we go for some pretty-to-guess passwords such as dates of birth, dates of wedding and names. This marginalizes your cybersecurity situation scenario because such types of passwords are easy to guess and break. To solve this problem, you should give your staff access to password management applications that can be seamlessly downloaded and installed across a number of mobile device platforms. As an owner of the firm, you should invest in the purchase of software and also the training of the employees. If you are using third-party applications such as Java and Adobe, you should do automatic updating of the operating systems and software to reduce the level of vulnerability.

Another weakness that tends to prevail over computer systems and networks is vulnerability of web applications. The following vulnerabilities can plague your webspace. On top of all is cross-site scripting, information leakage, security misconfiguration, structured query language (SQL) injection, leakage of information, loopholes in cryptography, problematic authentication, misconfiguration of security, and thin layers for protection.

There is a general perception among corporations and individuals that their websites and web applications are of little or no interest to attackers. Hewlett Packard's (HP) review different security assessments to calculate the level of security of web applications. The security teams at HP concluded that the viewpoint that corporation and individuals harbor is not right. Attackers don't think like that. They go on to say that apathy on the part of corporations and individuals invites the attention of attackers who infiltrate their systems without any resistance. It is these systems that play a key role in the proliferation of malware across computer systems in the world.

Social Media

Different corporations across the world and other nongovernmental organizations have employees on board who are constantly engaged in using social media tools. The military and universities are also replete with people who have a considerable presence on social media. These people can unknowingly create considerable problems for the organization or the institutions they work in. Any kind of mistake can result in embarrassment for the organization or loss of valuable financial resources. This mistake can be in the form of leakage of information by mistake. Certain risk assessment exercises are being done to estimate the range of risk that social media can expose organizations to. You can assign someone to develop a risk management strategy to identify the level of exposure to social media by the employees of an organization. A dedicated strategy will help assess the amount of potential risk and its effect on the organization.

Social media has become a sensation of the 21st century. There are a huge number of followers and users on social media. Their presence on social media has become almost ubiquitous. There is no chance that you can find the social media space empty of users. Some users are just swarming in the social media space for fun or to keep themselves updated on the latest developments but some of them take advantage of the information that is spread on social media platforms. The information that appears normal in the eyes of your employees to share on social media can do significant harm to the organization. On top of the social media networks are Facebook,

YouTube, Twitter, Vimeo, Picasa, Foursquare, Chatter, LinkedIn, and Chatter.

Your organization can suffer from damage to its reputation, defamation of a particular character, theft of identity, theft of intellectual property, theft of personal information, a potential malware attack on the computer network systems of the organization, and a potential compromise of confidential data.

Email Networks and Electronic Documents

Emails are usually considered as a gateway to personal information. In the United States alone, email is pretty prevalent across the corporate world. Consumers are encouraged to leave their email IDs for efficient communication and to give them an easy access to different products that are on sale online. The fact that creating and using an email ID is completely free has further complicated the process of communication. There are higher chances of loss of information and potential malware attacks.

As an owner of a financial consultancy firm, you can buy a service that tends to strip the IP location as well as metadata information from the emails you send to your customers or market competitors. Wherever the email travels on the internet, it will be more secure than before. You can also use certain services that have a kind of open-source software to ensure high-level security, compatibility and portability. You can also use private email accounts for your employees and their families to build up a cyber-safe-room for the coming decades to use.

Emergence of Cybersecurity

The computer has surfaced on the face of the world for a long time but since its inception, there was no considerable thought given to the need for the creation of a computer security program. There were engineers, physicists and scientists who worked on the creation of a computer network system. Their job was just to work on hardware and software of the computers. They didn't think about the possibility of invasions of cyberspace such as something like virus software. These challenges were completely ignored. At that time, one aspect of leakage of information was that someone breaks into a house and steals the hard disk drive of a computer. In the late 1980s, the aspect of cybersecurity surfaced and computer engineers and scientists started brainstorming ideas to ensure the security of the data stored on a computer. The security was put on a default mode in most devices. The security issues for software became apparent with the dawn of each day. Consequently, scientists developed the technique of encryption that could offer protection to data stored in the databases.

Dark Web

The dark web sounds scary and almost sends shivers down the spine of most people. The dark web is well-known for harboring illegal activity that lots of people don't want to engage in. The question starts spinning in our heads that if the dark web is a place for illegal activity, then why does it exist in the first place and who allows it to run without any kind of restrictions. Is there any purpose behind the existence and flourishing of the dark web or is the place being handled by a strong bunch of lot? There are three major parts of the internet known as deep web, surface web and dark web. Let me discuss each type individually and in detail.

The surface web consists of around ten percent of the entire internet, and it includes things such as Google and other search engines. You can use keywords to search different things to read, sell or buy. Then comes the deep web that is the place where you can store the information that is unavailable to most users. This includes things that you have protected by a password such as bank account subscription services as well as certain medical information. A majority of the webspace consists of this type of information. The third spot belongs to the dark web that is not accessible by a standard internet user. You cannot access this webspace through Firefox, Opera and Google Chrome, and it can have any kind of information. The word dark is attributed to this web space because of its limited accessibility.

You might be wondering if the dark web is completely illegal for a common user. Thankfully, the answer is no. Mere entering the dark web doesn't count as an illegal activity but what you do in the dark web can be categorized as legal or illegal. You can access the dark web through Tor anonymous browser. You can download it just like Google Chrome and Firefox. The difference is that it works in a different manner. You have to travel through different overlay networks when you are using Tor or The Onion Router. Just like an onion, it has a number of layers to pass through. The speed of Tor is usually slower than other browsers. If you can get your hands on a Virtual Private Network, it is better to ensure maximum security.

To clear the longstanding confusion, Tor is not a dark web but a tool to access the dark web. Also, Tor can be used to access general webspace such as Google and Yahoo and your travel through the surface web will be more secure. Rather than a place for illegal activities, the dark web is considered as a place for a high level of online privacy. You can buy illegal drugs through on the dark web and get them delivered to your postal address without giving anyone a hint to what was in the package. The ultimate objective to achieve by using dark web depends on what you need whether you are ready to take the risk of committing an illegal act.

Residents of countries such as Iran where the government control over the internet is touching extreme levels, the dark web becomes a necessity. Residents from these countries access Facebook and Twitter through the dark web. They log into their onion versions that have been officially launched for users who are subjected to censorship.

Chapter 2

Motivations Behind a Cyberattack

Cyberattacks are getting highly sophisticated as hackers are coming up with latest and innovative methods to stage an attack and threaten the security of different computer networks. The attacks are getting so much sophisticated that they are getting tougher to detect. Consequently, the attacks are getting more lethal than they were ever before. As per the latest statistics, cybercrime is rising across the world and according to estimates, the per-year cost of losses coming from cybercrime will touch a whopping $6 trillion by the time we enter 2021. (Cybercrime Damages $6 Trillion By 2021, n.d)

Cybersecurity doesn't depend on the size of your organization. Whether you have a start-up business or a multi-million dollar company, you should be able to be aware of how risky a cyberattack can be, The rise of cyberattacks gives room to the question of why do hackers attack a cyberspace? What is the motivation behind such heinous attacks? A general perception is that financial gain drives them to stage high profile cyberattacks on the computer systems of big corporations. Some also do that for espionage purposes. This chapter will shed light on the motivations that hackers have on their backs to penetrate an individual computer or an enterprise computer.

Most of the time, the attack is a kind of breach that aims at infiltrating the credit and debit card details. This information is then sold on the dark web later on to bag heavy profit. The story doesn't end here. In a majority of cases, profit is just a smokescreen to hide something bigger and deeper.

Espionage is also linked to a breach of data of a corporation or an official website of a country. These kind of attacks typically are aimed at retrieving information from the victim. There are lots of things that remain the same when it comes to espionage through a cyberattack, including monitoring of communication running on the cyberspace. There is another popular technique in espionage known as stealing secrets. Earlier on, this task came into the domain of individuals who physically penetrated the space and compromised certain assets that are found inside the organization. To give you a taste of how it all happened, I'll state an example from Hollywood. If you are a fan of Tom Cruise and his spy thrillers, you might for sure be acquainted with the character of Ethan who was always on some kind of mission to infiltrate a facility and steal some important documents that could turn the tables on the bad guys. Spy is the word that they use for such kind of person. Nowadays, things are different. There is hardly anything left in the physical domain. The craft of stealing an important bunch of information is more about being electric. Computers have the capacity to consume billions of files that were once stored in the company's ledgers and on loads of papers.

Espionage

Espionage attacks are getting more sophisticated nowadays. Most of them are state-sponsored or are financed by the corporate sector. Some professional groups act as independent contractors to spy for profit. Espionage is considered as a secretive activity in which attackers formulate a plan to avoid detection and achieve their objectives of collecting important information about the targeted company or individual. Spies are the most persistent attackers who keep on working until they achieve their objective. They keep on trying a number of techniques until they accomplish their mission.

Even if they are detected, they don't stop their activities and go on until the completion of the mission.

In most cases, the initial worker is indirect, such as a trusted third-party in the form of an employee who has access to the computer system you want to target. Once the attacker has access inside the system, he will have to move through the systems of the organization and also make his way to the data stores of the company. If you are running a financial consultancy firm, the most important data should be informed about your company's clients. Once the attacker has access to the documents, he will be in a position to blackmail you.

Profit

The second most common motivation of a hacker is financial gains. They aim at making heavy profits by the attack. The methods of profit-driven attackers vary. Usually, if the data stolen pertains to credit card and debit card details, it is understood that the objective of the cybercrime is financial gain. The information cybercriminals steal afterward sold on the dark web to make hefty profit. This is the greatest motivator in today's world in which locating the net worth of everyone is so easy. The transparency in financial transactions and details makes money as the single most important objective of a cyberattack. Everyone needs money and no shortage of cybercriminals wouldn't hesitate to share a pie from the money.

Different hackers use different types of methods that lead to some monetary gain. Cybercriminals use a wide range of methods using financial malware such as Dridex, Shifu, Carbanak, and Rovnix to siphon off loads of swag from the bank accounts of the victim. Another method to rob victims is to by using ransomware such as Tesla. Denial of service attacks (DDoS) is another profit-motivated attack that has become pretty top-notch in popularity over the past years.

Whether you are the owner of a consultancy firm or a retailer of clothes, you are at a high risk of a serious cyber threat if you conduct your transactions online. They are always after user and financial details that could lead him to the source of your finances as well as your customers' finances. If they loot you, you are devastated because you will not have precious capital to hold grounds. If they loot your customers, you will lose your hard-earned reputation in the market that is equally devastating for your business. In both ways, you are at great risk of losing your business. Attackers, at the height of rage, can use a malware that can target your point of sale (POS) systems.

Sometimes, profit alone is the sole objective of an attacker. For example, your company has secured a contract from Pentagon to produce sophisticated weapons and you are on your way to producing them. Hackers can target your company's database to compromise sensitive information that can be of strategic and police use of the attacker. The attacker can be a country that needs this strategic information to update her defense assets. It can be used by politicians to shape up their political campaigns. The chances are high that the state sponsors this kind of attack. Usually, states conduct this kind of classified mission through state-backed resources, but sometimes lack of resources can come in their way and they have to outsource this kind of mission to experts. Let's take a look at the most breached industries across the world.

Virtually all business are at a considerable risk of a cyberattack but some industries seem to be more vulnerable to these cyberattacks than the rest of the lot. The type of data that these companies hold makes them more vulnerable to cyberattacks. The very first industry on the line is the health industry.

Health

The health sector tops the list of cyberattacks in the United States and there are some valid reasons for that. The health sector carries personal information such as names, addresses, information about the income of people, social security numbers and email IDs. Hackers break into the databases at hospitals and access this information to exploit it later on. Their mode of attack is to gain a kind of unauthorized access to medical programs and an effort to get prescription drugs. Most of the threat has its origins inside the organization while some of the attacks are due to some kind of human error such as leakage of information about a patient by an employee of the hospital. The employee might not have suspected that the information could be manipulated by an individual or an organization. (Cybersecurity: the motivation behind cyber-hacks [Infographic], n.d)

Public Sector

The second vulnerable sector is public administration. Public administration such as government departments carry details about the employees such as names, addresses, bank account numbers and other personal information that can be compromised and misused if it comes in the hands of bad guys. Another reason why hackers highly target the public sector is that it suffers from a lack of funding in the cybersecurity realm that makes it weak and a potential target of cybercriminals. Personal information of high-ups and confidential information is at the top of the list of a hacker's to-do chart. Confidential information can be sold on the dark web for a heavy price. It can also be sold to a state for bigger profits.

(Cybersecurity: the motivation behind cyber-hacks [Infographic], n.d)

Financial Sector

The financial sector is another field that is most vulnerable to cyberattacks. Hackers relish at the personal information of the owners of hefty bank accounts. In addition, they can lay their hands on the credit card information of the clients of a finance firm.

Food Sector

The food industry is also in the line of industries that can be at great risk of cyberattacks. These businesses are quite vulnerable to certain breaches because they are always collecting credit card details of their customers, and their names and addresses. Once stolen, a hacker can use this precious information to steal the identity of a customer and gain unauthorized access to bank accounts. (Cybersecurity: the motivation behind cyber-hacks [Infographic], n.d)

Chapter 3

What Is Social Engineering
and How It Works?

Social engineering focuses on exploiting the weakest link in the security defenses of a particular organization, and that weakness is its employees. Yes, rather than adding to the strength of the organization they work for, the employees become their Achilles heel that gives the company a drag for a while. Social engineering is also known as people hacking as it spans around exploiting human beings who trust others without thinking much. Cybercriminals can use the information to break the security layers that the organization has set up to boost up its defense. This chapter intends to give you an insight into how a hacker can penetrate into your network by applying social engineering techniques. I will also give a couple of countermeasures to make sure you are not at the victim-end of a social engineering attack.

Hackers adopt a disguise to retrieve useful information that they couldn't access otherwise. When they have successfully obtained the information from the victims, they can wreak considerable havoc on the security systems of the organization by stealing confidential files or deleting them altogether. Social engineering is also used for industrial espionage or any other kind of heinous fraud to bring an organization onto its knees. A kind of revenge tactic, simply put. Social engineering is quite different from other physical security challenges, commonly known as dumpster diving. Let's take a look at the tactics that hackers use to accomplish social engineering.

- The very first tactic is becoming a false support official. A person can take up the disguise of fake support personnel to install new software on the computer system of a targeted user. He would talk the user into downloading the piece of software that would give them control over the entire computer system.

- The second method is to make a claim that you need to update the phone system of the organization. To achieve this purpose, you need to ask for the admin password that would give them complete access.

- Hackers would initiate a false contest that would allow them to collect IDs and passwords of the people who hop on to take part in the contest. When they have received usernames and passwords of the users, they would then go on to try those passwords on other websites such as Amazon and Alibaba to check out whether they work or not. Most people like to keep it simple and keep a single password for all websites. In this way, they can steal personal and financial information of unsuspecting users.

- The last technique is to take up the disguise of a false employee who would notify the security head that he has lost keys to his cabin. He would then get a set of keys and through the keys, access to the physical as well as an electronic information organization.

In some cases, social engineers are high-level employees, such as executives and managers. At other times, they take the role of naïve employees. When it comes to social engineering, basic communication between humans and their day-to-day interactions with other users have a considerable effect on the level of security of an organization. Social engineering is considered as one of the toughest hacks because it becomes pretty hard for an employee to portray himself as trustworthy to a stranger. It is equally tough to protect against because people have direct involvement in it. You cannot go out and protect all the employees against this kind of attack.

The Need for Social Engineering

Social engineering is an effective method that is used by hackers to break into a system after they have acquired the desired information. The only difference is that they don't actually break into the computer networks of the organization and risk getting caught. Instead, they use people to gain access to the information they need to hack into the security system. A social engineer cannot be stopped by firewalls, authentication devices, retinal scans, biometric security locks, access controls, and other devices that are deployed by the security team of your organization. Most of the time, social engineers tend to perform attacks at a slow pace that don't raise suspicion. They keep collecting chunks of information from the employees and then collect the pieces and form the complete picture that could guide them and help them infiltrate the organization later on.

If you cannot arrange an in-person meeting with the employee of the organization, you can go for the alternate methods of shooting an email or making a phone call to the person who is a potential target of the attack. The final decision on the choice of method belongs to the hacker who acts as he deems fit.

How to Perform a Social-Engineering Attack?

Social engineers need to find the details of the organizational process that they think will help them accomplish their objectives.

The information they receive helps them in pursuit of their objectives. The very first step is to have a clear goal of a social-engineering attack. Usually, hackers have an objective in mind. The next step is to build up a road map to achieve that objective. He may set his eyes on the intellectual property that you own, your passwords or the security badge of an employee of your organization to penetrate inside the facility and weaken the security system. Now let's take a look at the steps that hackers use to attain their objectives.

Collecting Information About the Victim

Social engineers start their operations by collecting important information about the victim. They do it slowly so that they might not flare up the spark of suspicion. They can use the internet to do it smoothly. For example, they can start in-depth research into the social media presence accounts of the victim. They give a few minutes to Google and find out how the person looks and what he likes. They can use the company name and search out the list of employees, their names and designations. Out of all the employees, they can single out their victims and gather important information about them.

The second method to collect valuable information about the victim is known as dumpster diving. It is pretty difficult to accomplish as a hacker has to go through trash cans to fish out information about the employee of the company. By this method, hackers can collect some confidential pieces of information. A majority of employees think that their information is safe inside the files that are in the office. After some time has passed, they almost forget about it. When the time comes to dispose of trash, the employees don't suspect how important a piece of paper is. They just throw it away without thinking about its value. These pieces of paper are literally trash most of the time and are of no value for an external person, but sometimes this is not the case. There is a treasure of information in these rubbish papers. For a social engineer, these pieces of information are no less than a key to open the gates of an organization for effective penetration.

There are some specific types of documents that become very lethal in the hands of a social engineer. For example, he can make good use of organizational charts, list of passwords, handbooks of employees, diagrams of computer network systems, minutes of meeting, reports, list of emails, and printed text or emails.

The only way you can minimize the threat of this kind of attack is by introducing the practice of shredding or incineration of the papers. Even shredders have different types. Some shredders cut papers into long strips that are basically worthless in front of a social engineer. With the help of a tape, he can join different pieces of paper and bring back a document to give it a thorough read. Proper shredding is needed.

There is another method using which hackers collect confidential information by eavesdropping the employees of an organization in restaurants, airports, subways, and coffee shops. Some people have a habit of speaking loudly into the telephones. They risk leaking some important information such as phone numbers or details about the network systems or firewalls. In their quest for information, hackers can go after discarded floppy disks, DVDs, CDs and hard disk drives or backup tapes.

The Trust Factor

This also is a very important factor in social engineering. Hackers will set on building trust with one of your employees. Humans by nature, love to trust others who are being nice to them. They go with the flow of events until something indicates that they shouldn't trust a particular person. People love to socialize and be part of a team. This human tendency is manipulated by hackers to access important pieces of information. Once they have built trust, they can easily attain their objectives. Hackers can achieve this milestone by being nice to their target. They exploit the human tendency to like a person who gives them a warm welcome and shows some courtesy or friendly attitude to them. They do this often by establishing some very common interests. When they conduct their research on their target, they note down their likes and dislikes and use this information, later on, to bridge the communication gap between them and establish trust. For example, if the victim likes roses or cars, you can share some valuable information with him or her. If she likes football, they will kick off small talk on the same topic.

Once they have established their likability in the eyes of the target, they can establish the belief factor by posing as a new employee who wants to make acquaintance with the old employees or as a vendor who is in constant business with the organization. They will do something nice to them first so that their image remains a positive one and the victim has compelling information with them under obligation.

Time to Exploit the Relationship

When a hacker successfully establishes trust with the victim, the next step to exploit this newly built relationship before the victim starts seeing through the covert designs of the hacker. Hackers try to coax them into providing them more information than they should have. This transfer of information should take place either in person during a coffee session or through electronic media. Whatever the medium of communication is, one thing that should be kept in consideration is that the victim must remain comfortable with the medium of communication.

Social engineers can retrieve important information from the victim in a number of ways, but the hot favorite of social engineers remains the use of catchy and captivating words and phrases. They would focus on keeping their conversations witty and funny, and would not give their victims time to think about. This also depends on the victim. If he is careless about what he is speaking, the job of a social engineer becomes really simple; otherwise, he has to adopt some cunning methods to accomplish his objective. Let's take a look at some common methods to make your victim say things that you want him to speak.

- You can act eagerly or overly friendly.

- You should mention the names of some executives or other prominent people in the organization to make the victim believe that you are an insider.

- You also brag about the level of authority that the victim enjoys in the organization.

- If the victim is a careless person, you can threaten him with dire consequences if he doesn't give you the desired information.

- Add some acting through gestures such as pursing your lips to show that you are nervous or anxious to know something. Make a conscious effort to control your feet and hands that are away from the face.

- You should appear to be in a rush so that the victim should have minimum time to open up his heart before you.

- Also, you should refuse to give some information that the victim is interested until the victim speaks first.

- It is always a better idea to know some key information about the company that usually an insider knows.

If you are communicating with the victim through written media, you can leave some words misspelled so that when the victim reads your message, he will go on explaining their meaning. In the effort of explaining the meaning, he may go on to give you more information that he had actually intended. These are some key tactics that a social engineer uses to retrieve important information when he is with the victim. Lots of people fall for one of the above tactics. They can also ask right away for a favor from the victim.

Another common tactic that social engineers use is to wear a disguise of an employee by dying the hair, wearing the same type of clothes, getting hold of a fake ID badge, or by simply dressing up like the employee. This works when the hacker is trying to infiltrate a big organization where thousands of employees work. The victim will feel that he has dressed up like us, has a badge like ours and even looks like us, and that's how he will start sharing the information that he otherwise wouldn't have. The hacker can demand a customer ID from the employee or any other piece of information such as the security codes.

Sometimes, a cybercrime through social engineering can be more lethal if it is done through a technical tactic. For example, you can create an artificial problem with the internet service of the victim and then jump in as the tech support guy to resolve the issue. Ask him about his old password and reset the password and tell him the new one. The unsuspecting victim will not heed what you have done with him. Through the password, you can enter his network system and get hold of some important pieces of information.

How to Counter It

Social engineering is a very cunning technique of committing cybercrime and sometimes it becomes quite a tough task to create a defense against such an attack. Even if you have proper security networks, a mistake by an unsuspecting employee can result in a compromising situation for your organization. A single mistake can let a hacker infiltrate the organization. However, there are some solid countermeasures, adopting which you can ensure that your organization will remain safe in the wake of cybercrime of this kind.

The first step is to classify the data you have in your office facility. The second step is hiring employees as well as contractors, and get them set up special IDs. Keep setting and resetting the password on your computer systems and network systems. You should handle confidential information with the utmost care, such as keeping it on a separate computer that cannot be accessed by all employees in the office. Guests should be properly escorted from the door to the cabin they intend to go so that they might not be able to take any piece of paper or other information if their intentions are malicious. If you leave the guests unattended, a hacker can enter the facility and roam around the office to access the database that can give you remote access to the network systems.

You should enforce these policies in your office so that you can secure your facility against any such attack. In addition, you need to sensitize your employees against a social engineering attack. Arrange a seminar, a workshop, a training session or a conference to educate them about the nature of this cyberattack and how to counter it. Ask your managers to keep an eye on the employees to find out the weak one who can possibly fall victim. When he or she has been detected, train them to fend themselves against such an attack. (Beaver, 2004)

Chapter 4

Cyber Terrorism
and How to Deal with It?

Cyber terrorism is not a new term and it has been around since the late 1980s. However, it saw its ascent since the September 11, 2001 incident. Cyber terrorism generally spans around hacking into public sector websites and portals, email bombs, attacking databases of hospitals, water departments, banking websites and other public sectors where attackers can find information about common citizens. In 2000, a hacker attacked Maroochy Shire, Australia waste management control system and pushed open the gates of a container that contained raw sewage. Millions of gallons of raw sewage went straight into a nearby town.

As the usage of the internet is rising each day, the trends of the terrorists are also witnessing a significant shift. They are now using cyberspace to use more traditional methods such as triggering bombs and fueling hate among communities. They have developed websites that are being used to convey their messages across, to coordinate their team members and also to recruit fresh members from across the world. Understanding the powerful effect of cyber terrorism, the United States, European countries and Asian countries have started taking viable steps to combat this new form of cyber terrorism.

What Is Cyber Terrorism?

The National Conference of State Legislatures define cyber terrorism in the following words:

> "[T]he uses of information technology by terrorist groups and individuals to further their agenda. This can include the use of information technology to organize and execute attacks against networks, computer systems and telecommunications infrastructures or for exchanging information or making threats electronically. Examples are hacking into computer systems, introducing viruses to vulnerable networks, web site defacing, Denial-of-service attacks, or terroristic threats made via electronic communication." (Cyber terrorism, n.d)

Cyberterrorist attack is not anything similar to staging a virus attack that would result in a denial of service for the user, but it is aimed at triggering physical violence or a kind of severe financial loss. The U.S. Commission of Critical Infrastructure Protection measures the severity and nature of attacks saying that the most vulnerable targets of cyber terrorists include power plants owned by the state, military installments, big banks and ground traffic control or air traffic control centers. If you have watched Die Hard 4 movie that has John McLane as a hero, you can easily understand how cyberterrorists can infiltrate firewalls and attack the traffic control centers to direct the flow of traffic so that they could navigate through the city and reach a specific destination or simply disrupt the flow of traffic in a city to create panic among citizens.

John McLane had to go through a similar situation. The villain of the movie turned out to be a computer genius who broke into the firewall and got control of the traffic and power plants into his hands. He turned off the power plants and jammed the traffic in the city to engage the city administration into clearing off the mess. Since he had the time now to do his job, he kicked off the mega plan to plunder millions of dollars. Thankfully, John met another computer genius who threw an ad bomb into the system of the villain that momentarily disrupted his computer network. The fight went on until the villain was shot dead. The movie showed how a single person could make the administration of an entire city hostage.

Cyber terrorism is also referred to as an information war. You should not get it confused with the term cybercrime. Cyber terrorism is different from cybercrime as terrorist groups execute it. It is a fact that the goals of both can be the same but the legal definitions for both terms are completely different. The scale of the intensity of the crime is different.

Types of Cyber Terrorism

Social networking has seen a great boom during the past few years because it has provided a platform for like-minded people to share their opinions regarding political, social, economic, and artistic points of view. People connect with one another and share their views irrespective of their geographical location. Cyberspace doesn't discriminate between people on the basis of color, race or location. This openness has created a free atmosphere that is sometimes misused by the bad guys. Cyber terrorism is a broad term that includes different types of attacks to harass people.

One of the major techniques to stage a cyber terrorism attack is by getting unauthorized access to a computer stealing files of staging a bigger attack from that platform. Lots of acts of cyber terrorism are similar to cybercrimes. This means that cyberterrorists and cybercriminals sometimes use the same methods, which makes it pretty hard to differentiate between the two.

Phishing is a kind of attack that involves sending fraudulent emails that convince the user that the sender is a legitimate fellow from a reputed organization. The main objective of phishing is to get private information such as identity theft, passwords and banking data. Another type of cyber terrorism is creating a watering hole. In this method, hackers deploy a fake webpage that compromises the original page. The visitors of the web page get deceived when they visit the age.

Ransomware is another method used by cyberterrorists. The main objective of this kind of method is to collect funds to finance their terrorist activities, such as bombings and killings. In a ransomware attack, hackers infect a system of an organization or an individual user with a kind of virus that locks down the system. If you are running a finance firm, you will not be able to access your computer systems and the operations will be jammed unless you make the payment to the hacking group.

One incident of a ransomware attack became quite famous. WannaCry attack was executed in May 2017 across the cyber world. It targeted computers that had been running on Microsoft Windows. The malware encrypted the data on the computer and demanded heavy ransom in return in bitcoin currency that doesn't leave a trace behind to find out the user.

Effects of Cyber Terrorism on Infrastructure

A cyberattack can have a wide range of objectives, such as economic disruption through infiltration into the financial networks. It can also be paired up with a physical attack to create an atmosphere of confusion so that the attention of the victim is divided. While they are busy in detecting the cyber-terrorist attack, the enemy will trigger a physical attack to overwhelm the victim. Cyberattacks have the potential to inflict financial loss worth billions of dollars and have affected the lives of countless people. Still, the world has yet to witness the implications of a truly catastrophic cyber-terrorist attack.

There are some direct cost implications of a potential cyber-attack such as loss of sales and customers during the time an organization has been suffering from a mega cyber-attack. The working hours will be disrupted which means that the staff is not working anymore. There will be certain network delays and your customers may not have access to your business during the time. The cost of insurance may increase due to the presence of litigation in the matter. You may become a victim of the loss of intellectual property. You will have to bear high costs for forensics for litigation matters. During the time of resolution of the issues, you may not be to communicate with the customers and the executives of the staff. There can be certain indirect cost implications such as a loss of confidence in your business by customers. You will lose credibility. This factor matters more if you own a financial consultancy firm. Your public image will be tarnished that is bad for your sales and revenue growth. If you have one or more business partners, your relationship with the business partners will see considerable disruption.

Countering Cyber Terrorism

Cyber terrorism is grabbing enormous attention due to the high amount of media coverage of the incidents that affected certain public and private sector institutions. Cyber terrorism has the potential to send panic waves at national and international levels. That's why it is the need of the hour to create awareness among people about this hot issue and let people defend themselves.

To counter this threat in an effective way, you need first to recognize who are cyberterrorists. Cyber terrorism can be inflicted by people harboring hostile intents and who also have the knowledge to use cyberspace to materialize their intentions. They can be amateur hackers or IT professionals. Sometimes disgruntled employees start playing in the hands of a hostile group or a terrorist group.

There are so many sources from which cyber terrorism threat can originate, which may create an impression that cyber terrorism is nearly impossible to stop, but that's not true. Cyberterrorist attacks are preventable, and by taking effective measures, you can significantly cut down the chances of cyberterrorist attacks.

Cyberterrorist attacks have some ulterior motives behind them such as the destruction of the operational capabilities of the enemy. Cyberterrorists deploy an attack to disable the operational capacity of the enemy. They will prepare a plan to disrupt the communication and networking system of the enemy to deprive them of effective communication for the conduction of smooth operations. Once, the normal everyday operations are disrupted, cyberterrorists can move on to the next plan to make the damage severe. These attacks have some pretty severe consequences in terms of economic and social matters. If cyberterrorists succeed in damaging some key business infrastructures and facilities, they can go on to affect the entire nation and business. For example, a mega attack on power plants of a country can bring public administration and business sector to a standstill. This is also extremely bad for the reputation of a nation because certain businesses and public sector corporations are highly reputed among the masses, and a mega level cyberattack on these facilities will send shock waves across the society. Even if cyberterrorist groups don't attack the power plants, they can jam the system by defacing the websites of major public sector and private sector organizations. By taking control of these websites, they get into a position to spread fake rumors.

Once they get control of their systems, cyberterrorists can compel the victims to switch their affiliation to certain parties. This is not an easy goal and can only be achieved if cyber terrorists get hold of a key database without which a business will come to a halt. These kind of attacks are highly motivated and can only be defended if the victim is ready to share information about its current state with its partners. Once they take their partners into confidence, they can be able to handle the situation skillfully and expertly.

Another motivation behind mega cyberattacks is to show their partners and followers that they have robust capability to inflict severe damage on the reputation of a nation or a business group. This kind of step strengthens their bond with their followers. It is a kind of reassurance of the leaders to the followers that they can do something big.

You can counter the damage inflicted by cyber-terrorism by making strategic plans to ensure the health of your business. The very first approach is to shed any impression of fear or intimidation and come out in the forefront to tackle the perpetrators and to take them to task. Purse the perpetrators by finding them and holding them accountable as per the law. If the cyberterrorist group resides out of the country, the attempt may be futile yet it will be to the advantage of the organization. If you have identified the group behind the attack, you can easily locate them or keep their record for future reference. If the attack is repeated, you can initiate prosecution and bring the perpetrators of the attack to justice. Initiation of investigation and trial can compel the cyber-terrorist groups to mend their ways out of the fear of prosecution and jail time. If a decision comes while they are in another country, the victims can request for an extradition or at least the judgment can ensure that the attacker cannot fly into the country whose court has decided against him. In this way, we can control the number of cyberterrorist attacks.

Another countermeasure is to ensure that you should develop and then implement a set of the best security practices that suit your operations. They can include a coordinated effort by all the members of the organization, meaning that all the staff members and department heads should adopt standard practices to ensure security. As an owner of an organization, you can adopt standard security practices such as ISO17799. These standard practices give you detailed steps to follow to beef up the security environment in your organization. You should keep modifying the security standards as per shifting needs. In addition to this, you can also improve the security guidelines to suit the changing security environment.

Cyberterrorist attacks demand a proactive approach by the heads of organizations. Being proactive while tackling cyber terrorism demands that your financial firm must remain up to date with respect to the latest developments in the security realm such as the introduction of new anti-virus software and the latest types of malware and the measures to counter them. In addition, you should be determined to update your security networks so that the chances of penetration are minimum. Organizations should improve their current security network infrastructure by eliminating what has been outdated and integrating what is new in the market. In addition, there should be multiple security layers in the organization for better insulation against cyberattacks. You should develop a system of running security audits inside the organization to assess the level of threats in the organization. Organizations should also look forward to improving the existing security infrastructure by adding multiple tiers such as physical tiers and online tiers.

One of the most important countermeasures to tackle a cyberterrorist attack is that in the wake of attack, you should be able to run your business as usual and set the course of your business on recovery in no time. Your organization should include a fast emergency response system that runs the business in safe mode so that you be saved from bearing the full brunt of the incident. This will help you save your customer base and also improve the image of your organization in the market. Your customers and competitors will hail your organization as the one that is resilient to any kind of cyberterrorist attack. This proactive approach is crucial if you are running a defense industry that has contracts from the government to make weapons. If a cyberterrorist attack succeeds in bringing your organization down to its knees, you will have to live up with this shame in the years ahead, not good for the reputation of your organization. The two plans should span around two major things that are reparation of the loss and restoration of the system to its healthy state.

You should run a general awareness program in the organization to sensitize the employees on the importance of security and the dire sequences that the company has to face in the wake of an attack. Employees should be trained to defend themselves against such kind of attacks. This kind of awareness will help develop a kind of community that would be more proactive in dealing with a number of security issues. Different types of security training programs can equip people with the skills they need to protect their computer systems and networks.

At the government level, strict cybersecurity laws should be in place. The government can restrict certain websites and social media platforms that it thinks would affect the security environment in the country. New laws can be enacted to make sure that everyone in the country is secure.

Chapter 5

Cyber-Espionage and
Its Geopolitical Repercussions

Cyber-espionage is an act of getting engaged in an attack that allows an authorized user to view classified material. Cyber-espionage attacks, in general, are quite subtle and may comprise of a single piece of code that goes unnoticed in most public sector offices. It can be a process that has the power to run in the background of a workstation or a computer in an office. Usually, the target is a corporate or a public office. The major goal of a cyber-espionage attack is to grab hold of some intellectual property or classified secrets from the government. The attackers have several motivations for planning and executing an attack. They can do it in return for hard cash or gold or some other benefits such as freedom of their companions from prisons. The last motivation works when a government is trying to spy on the government of another country. Its consequences can be bad such as loss of strategic advantage if the cyber-espionage is being executed by a government and loss of competitive advantage if a corporation is executing the cyber-espionage against a corporation.

This chapter will explain what cyber-espionage is and how devastating it can be for the people of different countries and corporations around the world. It will also explain the geopolitical and geostrategic repercussions of a cyber-espionage attack against a government or a strategic industry. Generally, espionage is defined as a practice of using spies to get information about the activities and plans of a government and corporations.

For cyber espionage, the spies are generally an army of nefarious hackers that are recruited from different countries of the world. These cyber-spies or malicious hackers are experts in political, economic, and military domains. These high-level cybercriminals are equipped with the latest tech knowledge for shutting down key government structures such as banks and other such utilities. They have the power to influence elections and disrupting international events such as summits and formal meetups.

Top Spying Tactics

For a good number of years, there have been attempts to seek benefits by illegally knowing what the competitors are doing. Naturally, a company needs reconnaissance of its competitor just as a country needs information on the other country's activities. One of the most common tactics to run a viable espionage campaign is to hire people to send in as faux employees who would attempt to access key pieces of information on specific projects. The faux employee will gain access to a certain project that is being developed with the help of the latest technology.

Faux employee technique is quite useful but it is a bit risky because the other company's security team may detect an aberration in the behavior of the employee or catch him doing any other suspicious activity. For the past few years, another tactic has replaced it. Now companies lookout for an unsecured workspace and then hire someone who can go in as a guest and casually stick in a USB drive on one of the computers or the main server to upload a worm or a malware. The virus will be transferred in a matter of seconds. The main purpose of this tactic is to flip open a secure portal and then exploit it so that you can target it later on from a remote location. The virus in the USB drive will give you enough control over the computer network from a remote site that you can get into the system and inflict whatever damage you want on the system.

Certain business websites offer some kind of opening portal that can be later on exploited by an experienced hacker. Many business websites are not secured up to a standardized level. Hackers can use it to enter the server of the business and steal whatever data he requires. Moreover, there is usually a list of email IDs of the employees of a company. Hackers can use these email IDs to shoot emails to the employees with a line of code or a link inside to lure the employees into clicking a suspicious link that would not do any harm apparently but is lethal enough to enable the perpetrator of the attack to plan a lethal attack later on. This is what we called spear phishing.

A Look at Cyber-Espionage Affairs

Espionage is usually conducted among nations of the world, and it is not a new phenomenon. It is in place since the medieval period and it has only been upgraded from time to time and so are the spies. Cyber-espionage among nations is a new phenomenon and a lethal one. Countries use cyber-espionage to gain military, political and economic advantages over their competitors. Countries recruit highly-skilled individuals for the preparation of a customized espionage plan that could inflict some serious damage on their enemy. At extreme levels, a cyber-espionage attack can shut down a public sector infrastructure or a military infrastructure of the victim country. At a slightly lower level, it would target the financial institutions of the country and disrupt the process of state banks, certain financial transactions and stuff like that. In short, cyber-espionage has the capacity to bring down the systems of all the countries of the world that are connected to the internet. There will be complete chaos if no country tries to resist it. The worst thing about cyber-espionage that also is the best thing about is its tendency to give foolproof cover to the perpetrator of the attack. Hackers behind these attacks have the power to rub their footsteps. This threat is now extending its arms to multiple domains such as education, production and public offices.

An Overview of Some Latest Cyber-Espionage Attacks

On top of all, the cyber-espionage attacks that happened in 2019 is the Chinese and Iranian hackers' attack on the US agencies. The news has recently surfaced that Iranian and Chinese hackers attacked businesses and certain public offices in the United States. Experts believe that these attacks happened after Donald Trump announced withdrawal from the nuclear deal of Iran and the initiation of the biggest trade war with China that affected billions of dollars of trade. The US intelligence chief reported that these countries deployed hackers to steal information from the United States and to influence the opinion of the public in the United States and also to derange strategic infrastructure in the country. According to the assessments of the intelligence officials, the major objective of the hackers was to gain a foothold in the networks to position themselves to carry out future attacks. (9 Latest Cyber-Espionage Affairs, Mar 7)

Another significant incident of the year happened in Pakistan when the country's website of the Ministry of External Affairs was hacked and its access to different countries got restricted. People in Pakistan could see and visit the website but citizens of Britain, Holland, and the Kingdom of Saudi Arabia faced serious issues with respect to accessing the website. Finally, a detailed investigative report revealed that the source of the attack was in India. The incident happened right after the Pulwama attack in India. (9 Latest Cyber-Espionage Affairs, Mar 7)

Kaspersky Lab exposed Slingshot in 2018. Most of the victims of the attack were in the Middle East and Africa. The primary objective of the Slingshot attack was to take screenshots of the computer screens of the victim, collect keyboard data, passwords, and network data. Later on, the US intelligence men accepted that slingshot was developed and loaded by the US military as part of an official program to track down terrorists and retrieve important data from them. (9 Latest Cyber-Espionage Affairs, Mar 7)

Countries can defend themselves against any kind of cyber-espionage attempt by partnering with security experts. In this way, they can fully understand the extent of the threat and can also counter it effectively. The public or corporate officials can point out the assets that need foolproof protection. You should also indicate what the vulnerabilities are in your system. It is also better to run a security risk assessment test to pinpoint the weak areas in your official or corporate sector systems. Once you know what the vulnerabilities are, you can go on to fix them right away. This data will give you an insight into how to develop an in-depth strategy.

Chapter 6

Cyberwarfare and
How to Defend Against It?

Cyberwarfare alludes to the use of technology for launching attacks on governments, corporations, and citizens of a country to inflict significant harm. There are generally no weapons involved in the warfare, and all this happens in the cyber world. There has been much talk about cyberwarfare across the globe but the fact remains that there is not a single cyberwar that has declared antagonists. Still, there is no shortage of incidents that have caused somewhat serious disruption to the infrastructure and that experts suspect have been perpetrated by a state.

The Oxford English dictionary's definition of cyberwarfare is: "The use of computer technology to disrupt the activities of a state or organization, especially the deliberate attacking of information systems for strategic or military purposes."

Cyberwarfare is tricky because at the time of the incident, people have no idea who has started the attack and why is he doing that? There are lots of question that are spinning in the heads of public office holders but only a few answers. Sometimes there are no answers at all. This creates a giant web of confusion among people; that's why the very first reaction to this kind of situation is silence. In a majority of cases, no one steps up to claim responsibility for the attack. Countries can open the doors of speculation on the basis of raw guess and current geopolitical situation, but there are no concrete accusations. The reason behind the absence of any tracks is that the states are quite deft at brushing them off on the back of enormous resources and availability of expert talent. Also, you cannot prove that a state is directly involved in the attack, even if you can track down the perpetrators. The hackers can be individual contractors that have been hired by a state on the condition that they will not disclose who had hired them for the job.

Still, some stories keep circulating across the states about cyberwarfare, and some of them are quite scary. What will happen if state-sponsored hackers will have enough power to blackout the entire world by executing multiple cyber-attacks across the country? What if they will infiltrate banks and freeze different ATM machines across countries to jam the flow of cash? Perhaps they will succeed in shutting down the airports and shipping firms. Ports will be closed and factories will be put under lockdown because hackers will take control of the power plants. They will go on to paralyze airports as well as hospitals. All these scary stories start floating across the world whenever some mega attacks happens in the world.

In fact, sometimes, we have got to see these scenarios as they are no longer hypothetical, and they have started happening. Cyberwarfare has materialized these stories. Once, it was a thought or a mere fantasy that hacking could disrupt entire systems of the state rather than being just a tool for plunder and loot, but now we see that hacking can really disrupt states' operations.

A good news is that so far, cyberwarfare has not resulted in any kind of direct loss of life, but it is a truth that cyberwarfare has shown us that it can inflict significant financial loss. Cyberwarfare has been used to create panic among the industrial sector. Up till now, it has been used to deny civilians access to some basic services such as power and heat. With changing geopolitical scenario, it has been observed that smaller countries that feel being bullied by the bigger powers seem to be trying out cyber warfare to flex their muscles in this realm. Iran, Russia and North Korea seem to be keen on using cyberwarfare to equal the power of mighty countries such as the United States because they know that they cannot match her in the traditional warfare. Still, it is a fact that the United States has the most advanced cyber warfare capabilities in the world. It is just that she is showing a bit more restraint to keep the situation in hands.

A Brief History of Cyberwarfare

If we want to understand what cyberwarfare is and how it started, we should give a brief read to its origins. It is worth understanding how the world is defining this. The term itself is decades old and was first chronicled in Thomas Rid's history Rise of the Machines. There were talks of automatic weapons and flying cars. Then came the idea of robotic warfare with the concept of a terminator who goes on a killing spree. In 1993 the think tank RAND floated the idea of how military hackers would be used in future for attacking the computers of the enemy that they were using for command-and-control.

The prospect of a full-on cyber war evolved with the rise in IT power of China, the United States, and Russia. There are lots of other countries such as North Korea, Iran and Saudi Arabia that have already hopped on the bandwagon. Cyberweapons are getting more sophisticated with the dawn of each day. They are now more aggressive and fast as states have been backing them with huge resources. So far, a mega cyber-attack on critical infrastructures of countries has not happened but the possibility of an attack in the near future cannot be ruled out.

Russian, China and Iran are seen as making considerable progress in the field of cyberwarfare to break the hegemony of the United States in the world. They are now inching toward challenging the status of the United States by defeating her in the cyber world, knowing that the United States leads the world in the domain of cyberwarfare. Where these three countries are moving toward fulfilling their designs, the United States is also creating a robust and offensive-oriented cyber doctrine that would turn out to be a super tough shield in the wake of an attack, and would also prepare a powerful response in a short span of time. This competition tells us that cyber warfare is going to change its way and become more aggressive and destructive in the near future.

There have been a conflict of interests and an enormous difference of opinion among world powers. Russia dislikes the policies of the United States and she has been pushing forward the idea of the so-called national sovereignty. Kremlin is frustrated because the United States is ever ready to combat any plan to challenge its writ. In addition, Russia hates freedom of speech and she dislikes the meddling of the United States to support freedom of speech across the world. Russia has gone to the extent of saying that it would cut off from the global internet and form its own national internet if the United States didn't stop

Russia and the United States have also been engaged in probing each other's power sectors. Experts suspect that they might have succeeded in planting malicious codes into the systems so that they can control the power sectors if an all-out war breaks out. China is not lagging behind in the cyber world. She harbors the same ambitions as Russia as she appears to be fed up with the unilateralism of the United States. China, just like Russia, loves the idea of state censorship. She is blocking access to lots of international websites, and she also wants to follow the idea of a national internet. It has executed multiple crackdowns on anti-government speeches on the internet.

49

There is a third factor that has significantly changed the equation of cyberwarfare. Iran is also fed up with the hegemony of the United States, and she wants to inflict damage on the United States from behind the scenes.

An Overview of Weapons Used in Cyberwarfare

Russian and China are on their way to developing sophisticated cyber weapons for future usage. Similarly, the United States, Israel, and France are also very active among the nation-states in leading the way in the cyber world. Well, this doesn't prove that all these countries have started using cyberweapons against other countries, but they can use them if they get caught in a conflict with one another. If we can recall, Stuxnet was a joint venture of the United States and Israel to reverse the progress of the nuclear program of Iran.

Cyberweapons used by the state are no different than the weapons used for criminal attacks by hackers. Social engineering that I have already dedicated a chapter to is one of the few cyber weapons to be used. Stuxnet was a perfect example of a cyber weapon. It was discovered in 2010 and was made of multiple layers of attack to ensure maximum loss on the part of the enemy. The manner it happened is still a matter of debate among cybersecurity experts, but a majority of them agree that it was a USB that someone either knowingly or unknowingly inserted into an air-gapped system and it infected the Iranian nuclear power programmer pushing it decades behind from where it has reached. The malware in the USB drive made use of multiple zero-day exploits and was made as such to hunt down the software that ran and controlled the centrifuges. Once it had located the software of centrifuges, it spans them faster than its normal speed and that too in an undetected manner. The speed of the centrifuges remained faster than normal for a period of several months and eventually, the centrifuges broke. Stuxnet affected around one 1000 machines.

No one officially claimed responsibility for the attack but people across the world believe that it was a state-sponsored program and a joint venture by the United States and Israel. The interesting thing is that no country that was accused denied the attack. Stuxnet is an all-time famous example of a lethal cyberweapon that silently killed the nuclear power programmer of Iran inflicting a loss of millions of dollars on Iran.

Another example comes from Russia that remains accused of several state-sponsored cyberattacks. Russia has faced accusations of designing and mounting some pretty grave cyberattacks against Ukraine. The most notorious of the attacks is the BlackEnergy attack that resulted in rendering around 700,000 houses without power in 2015. Another one is the NotPeya malware that turned out to be ransomware but in reality, it was made as such to destroy the computer systems it infected.

North Korea has also been in the news for its cyberattacks. It has a turbulent relationship with the United States at the diplomatic especially because the latter is an adamant opponent of its nuclear programmer. North Korea doesn't have the power to compete in the United States at the economic and even the nuclear level so it has taken this new approach of competing in cyberspace. Cyber experts say that North Korea has been involved in some pretty dangerous cyberattacks. They have tried to form a link between North Korea and the Lazarous Group. The most notorious of the attacks that had generated news headlines for the days to come was the attack on Sony Pictures entertainment.

Hackers broke into the network of Sony Pictures Entertainment and stole a huge amount of confidential documents from their office and afterward posted them online in the coming weeks. This exposed the documents to the masses from journalists and common people to cybercriminals who could possibly use the information to maximize their financial gains. Journalists poured through the huge amount of documents and reported almost everything the papers contained. Most of the documents carried details of a recent film by Sony Pictures Entertainment but there were plenty of papers that exposed the data of the employees.

There were more than one report by the US government that linked the cyberattack to North Korea, and there were pretty solid reasons to think so because North Korean government had shown displeasure toward Sony Pictures because of a film it had produced. The film, named The Interview, was an action-comedy that revolved around an assassination plot of Kim Jong Un, the ruler of North Korea.

What actually happened in Sony Pictures was creepy, to say the least. The employees of Sony Pictures reached their office one Monday morning and tried to log into their computer. They were taken aback from what they had seen on the screen. There was a picture of a neon red skeleton that greeted them. The screen showed them the following words: #Hacked by #GOP. The group threatened Sony Pictures to release a huge amount of data if the company officials didn't accept their request. There was more than one statement from the GOP group.

Each message from the Guardian of Peace group accompanied links to download the data that they had stolen from Sony Pictures networks. The day the attack happened, the FBI released a memo warning companies about the entry of a new kind of malware. Even after the passage of days and weeks, the employees at Sony Pictures couldn't log into their old computers because the company officials were not sure if they had completely removed the malware from the system or not.

The government of North Korea didn't claim the attack and that's why attribution to a specific group or individual was tough, but officials and the vast majority of cybersecurity experts linked the attack to the North Korean government. North Korean officials denied the responsibility for the attack but dubbed it as a righteous deed and cherished it. It also alluded to the fact that the group that committed the act might have been among the group of supporters of the regime. The responsibility couldn't be imposed on a specific person or government but North Korea gave an indication that it supported the act of the hacking group.

Defending Against Cyberwarfare

Cyberwarfare has considerably evolved over the past few years from being a theoretical concept to a practical thing. The destructive nature of cyberweapons has been growing at a lightning-fast pace, thanks to the rising ace of cyberattack tools and cyber mercenary groups.

Cyberweapons can inflict unprecedented damage to the economic infrastructure of a country. Now the warfare has changed its shape and it is being conducted in the cyber realm. Military leaders are now brainstorming to create new lines of defense against the attacks in cyberspace. They are now developing intelligent systems to safeguard their assets that remain in the cyberspace.

There has been a significant rise in the number of cyberattacks, and now hackers have access to an arsenal of powerful and automated cyber weapons. The weapons range from denial of service attacks to dictionary attack weapons that are designed as such to try out a wide range of password combinations to log into a network system.

Another method is social engineering that revolves around harvesting key information from the employees of a government or a corporation.

The scale of the destruction of a cyber weapon is so wide that it is pretty hard to calculate what amount of loss it is capable of inflicting. For example, the WannCry ransomware infected around 300,000 computers in around 150 countries. The number of affected computers was great and the radius it covered was amazing, to say the least.

The enormity and vastness of the attack have made defenses against these kinds of attacks a matter of great concern. Militaries around the world are now preparing themselves for a new battlefront. They have started to understand by now that it is not just a matter of technological race but a question of how much resources do you have and how brilliant is your manpower. It requires considerable time and hours long coding to assess the source of an attack and the solution to prepare a solid defense to the attack. That's where the problem lies. Militaries around the world have hardly the manpower that is required to carry out such kind of attacks. In fact, there has been a serious shortfall of cybersecurity workers around the world.

From the Sony Pictures attack, we can deduce the fact that it is not easy to respond to a cyberattack right away. In fact, it is difficult to guess the timing of the attack. When Sony Pictures employees saw the screen created by the hackers, all the documents had already been stolen and uploaded on the internet. The screen was just a kind of intimation that they had been attacked. They might not have known about the attack had the hackers not displayed the message on the screens.

The first problem is the detection of the attack. In some cases, the attack is visible. For example, if the cyberattack is made on a power plant, it is easier to detect. Still, it takes considerable time and effort to locate the origin of the attack and even if you find out the origin of the attack, it is hard to fix responsibility on a government if the latter doesn't claim it or outright deny it.

There have been attempts by countries to beef up defenses against a potential cyberattack. One such example of preparation for cyberwarfare is the Locked Shields exercise that NATO has been running for quite some time. There is a country names Berylia in the scenario that is a fictional member state of NATO and has been floating in the North Atlantic. This state has a somewhat tough relationship with Crimsonia, the rival state. Crimsonia is supposed to be located near the eastern side of Europe. The project is being operated by the Cooperative Cyber Defense Center of Excellence of NATO and is currently the largest and one of the most complex international technical defense exercises that involve around 900 participants from a total of 25 nations.

Each year a bunch of national teams participates in the games, out of which one is from NATO itself. NATO has been conducting this kind of exercise for the past few years and this has made it crystal clear that cyberwarfare is no more a fantasy and it has moved from the theoretical realm to the practical realm. Not just NATO, individual countries are also spending a huge amount of sum on improving their capacity to defend themselves in the wake of cyberwarfare and also to come back with an overwhelming response to deter and defeat the enemy. The United States, China and Russia top the list of the nations that boast of some pretty advanced capabilities in the field.

The 2015 hacking attack on the power sector of Ukraine that had left hundreds of thousands without power turned out to be a wakeup call for governments around the world. The attack showed the potential of a cyber weapon and its importance in a traditional warfare. Just imagine if a country loses all its power amidst a traditional attack by its neighbor. It means complete annihilation or surrenders in a matter of hours before the enemy. How embarrassing it is! In fact, how destructive it can be for the world! The country that has the most sophisticated cyber tech can wipe out the other countries or make them its slave.

Since the attack on Ukraine's power sector, countries have started giving full attention to the importance of the development of cyber weapons and defenses. Just like every year, this year the teams were given the task to protect Berylia's major military airbase from any kind of cyberattacks. The contending teams have to defend everything thing on the base such as the main office, the personal computers that had Windows operating systems, Mac operations system, Linux operations system, email accounts and all the major or minor servers. The teams were also given the task to defend the systems that controlled the power sector and the office that controlled military air traffic. Other facilities that came under the defense were military surveillance drones and the control offices that directed the fuel of supply to and from the airbase. The basic idea behind the exercise was to reinforce the concept that all individual systems and office that are inside or outside of the facility but are somehow linked to it should be protected as they can be a potential target of the hackers.

The Locked Shields exercises have expanded their realm and have turned into a sort of communications game. The teams have started to respond for certain interviews to update the people about how their response to a certain attack went. It has become a kind of game in which participants have to deal with a pack of threats and neutralize them in a short amount of time. Each team has a different set of threats and it depends on its decisions on how well it will protect the state of Berylia.

The teams are assigned different colors and different PCs. Red denotes the attackers while green denotes the infrastructure team that has the responsibility to keep the game in the running mode. White is the color given to the team responsible for the communications as well as legal teams and others that are running inside the scenarios.

There is a bunch of people who are encouraged to act as naïve people who unsuspectingly click on suspicious links and welcome all kinds of viruses into their system that allows the attackers to initiate a lethal cyberattack against the defenders. So the defenders are deliberately put in a difficult situation so that their appetite can be tested. The users who have suffered from a cyberattack has the facility to file a complaint with the blue team that they are unable to access their email and other services because they have just clicked on a ransomware and are now unable to open anything on their own computer. This creates another hassle for the defending team to deal with and resolve.

The games are designed as such to introduce a new set of viruses and a unique kind of threat each time it starts to give participants a taste of how a real cyberattack happens and what should be their response to it. That's how they are able to develop a unique strategy each time to deal with the threat. The environment is just so real that everyone is greatly involved in what is happening. This makes these games efficient when it comes to create a defense shield against a cyberattack.

This kind of exercises will enable countries to respond to a cyberattack in real-time and also to neutralize an attack right at the source of at least right after it has been triggered. The main objective is to minimize the amount of time that was earlier spent on detecting the nature of the threat and then creating a response to deal with it. (Ranger, 2017)

Chapter 7

An Overview of Ethical Hacking

Times are changing fast. The advent of technology has transformed the nature of threats and attacks and also the strategies to deal with them. This changing nature of threats has demanded a shift in the approach on behalf of business owners as well. Nowadays, corporations have been suffering from serious threats from cybercriminals. Their data is at risk and their financial transactions are also vulnerable to an attack by hackers.

Traditionally, a hacker was considered as an individual who would illegally tinker with the software and databases of a company to make illegal monetary gains. Hackers enjoyed the anonymity the cyberspace offered to them, and they went on to explore the documents and files of certain businesses without their prior permission. They have become a sort of evil force nowadays and have become someone who would harbor evil intentions and also break into systems of corporations to steal important data or to disrupt the flow and directions of financial transactions. That's how they take up the position to blackmail owners of a corporation and demand monetary benefits in exchange for leaving their system alone. The intentions of hackers nowadays are mostly malicious. Either they need financial gains or they are working for an arm of a government or acting as an individual contractor who would do a job in return for money. Some hackers are bent on becoming famous on the back of committing these malicious acts while some of them are bent on taking revenge. The attack on Sony Pictures of which I have explained in detail was an act of revenge on the company for making a movie on Kim Jong Un that intended to mock him.

All hackers are not the same. Some white hat hackers would work to counter the acts of black hat hackers and ensure property security for your cyberspace. Ethical hacking has been the talk of the town for quite some time. Ethical hackers ensure that your cyberspace is perfectly secure in the wake of any hacking attack. It aims at removing any kind of loopholes and weak points from the security framework in your organization.

This chapter explains what ethical hacking is and why it is necessary to ensure foolproof cybersecurity in your organization. Most people give hackers a negative attribution and ethical hacking goes on to change this perception of the people. The point is that you need protection from cyberattacks. An ethical hacker would offer you the skills, the mindset and the right tools that would ensure cybersecurity in your organization. An ethical hacker has all the same tools that a malicious hacker has. The only difference is that an ethical hacker is more trustworthy and use them for positive purposes. Ethical hacking is also known as penetration testing or white-hat hacking. Ethical hacking is completely legal as a company hires a hacker to test its security layers and find any possible loopholes that can be exploited by the bad guys. It is only legal if you take prior permission from the owner of the organization to test its security networks. It is a kind of information risk management program that creates room for improvement in the security environment. Ethical hacking can clear the air about doubts in the security networks of an organization. Ethical hackers also offer you viable solutions for key security problems in an organization.

A Look at the Dangers Your Systems Face

To know that your system is vulnerable to cyberattacks is one thing and to know what kind of dangers you are facing is another thing. You should be specific when it comes to explaining the dangers against your system. Experts believe that many information-security weaknesses are hardly critical; however, exploiting the weaknesses can take its toll on the security of your security networks. Some weaknesses are so minute that they are almost negligible in your eyes. They include a weak SQL Server password, a default configuration of the operating system on your computer and also a server on your wireless network. If a hacker opts to exploit all these vulnerabilities at the same time, this can turn out to be a serious issue for your organization.

A hacker can attack the network infrastructure in your organization. Nowadays, network systems are interconnected and a remote hacker can access your system from anywhere in the world if you are connected to the internet. He can connect to the network with the help of a rogue modem that is attached to a computer inside a firewall. He can exploit the weakness in TCP/IP and NetBIOS that are generally considered as network transport mechanisms. They can flood your network system with overwhelming requests and can also create a denial of service attacks. They can download and install a network analyzer on your network and watch every packet of data that travels to and from your system. This really compromises the data that travels inside the system. It can provide financial details of your clients such as their business details, their net worth, their credit card details and many other things. They can retrieve all the information in the form of clear texts.

Another popular method is to initiate an operating system hacking attack. Operating systems make up a significant portion of the attacks by hackers because they contain one or more loopholes that you can exploit later on. It is a fact that the strength of operating systems varies. For example, Linux is considered more secure than a Windows operating system or Mac operating system. Still, Linux is also one of the most targeted operating systems because it is one of the most widely used operating systems across the world.

Hackers would exploit protocol mechanisms in the operating system. They would attack the authentication systems and break into the file-system security. In addition, hackers would crack passwords and encrypt a wide range of mechanisms. Apps are another field that remain under attack by hackers.

What Is The Ethical Hacking Process?

Ethical hacking, like any other security project, needs advance planning. Hackers need to determine certain strategic and tactical aspects of a hacking episode. Planning is considerably important for any kind of testing from checking the strength of a password on your administrator computer to a full-fledge penetration test of your entire security framework.

In the entire planning set up, the very first thing is the formulation of your plan. You need to need to get approval for hacking a system. You need to make sure whatever you do should remain visible to the decision-makers at the company. Ethical hacking is aimed at knowing the weaknesses and strengths of the company in the wake of a cyberattack. If a professional white-hat hacker conducts it, it adds to the security of the system. One crucial aspect of ethical hacking is that no one should have knowledge of whether a penetration testing is being conducted on the system or not. Only the owners of the company or a bunch of executives should have the knowledge so that someone may not call off the testing in the middle of the process.

You can circulate an internal memo inside the organization to intimate the people who should know about the initiation of an ethical hacking test. After that, there should be a detailed plan to execute the attack. It means that you need a number of volumes of testing procedures. The hacker should include the following in the plan.

1. The systems you need him to test, such as the server computer or any other computer that you consider at a high risk of a cyberattack.

2. The hacker should calculate and bring into written form the risks that are involved in the wake of an attack.

3. The hacker should perform multiple tests to check the performance of the system.

4. The hacker should measure the performance of tests and their impacts on the system.

5. He should measure what amount of knowledge you have before you start testing

6. The hacker should be ready to deal with any kind and level of vulnerability in the system before he initiates the testing.

7. The hacker should include a security-assessment report and also a high-level report to outline the general weaknesses that need to be addressed. He should also formulate certain countermeasures that need to be implemented to minimize any real cyberattack on the system. The recommended countermeasures should be adopted to ensure maximum security. If you don't adopt the countermeasure, you will

remain at a disadvantage, and the whole purpose of the ethical hacking episode will fail to deliver.

When you are selecting systems for testing, you need to start with the most vulnerable systems in the company. For example, you can test computer passwords or plan a social engineering attack before you go down deep into more complex systems. Don't forget to demand from your hacker to keep a contingency plan in place in case the ethical hacking test goes awry. For example, your firewall may show some serious weaknesses when the hacker tries to test it out. As a result, it falls flat on its face, exposing your organization's security frameworks to considerable weakness. Your web application will be taken down and this can create serious unavailability of systems for your customers. System performance will slow down and your employees' productivity will start touching the bottom levels. You can lose data and welcome some pretty bad publicity in the market. That's why a contingency plan should be in place for each kind of attack you initiate.

In addition to other attacks, you need to handle social engineering attacks with the utmost care. Hackers should be able to determine how these attacks can affect the systems of your organization. The best approach to ensure foolproof security is to stage an unlimited attack that encompasses different types of attacks inside your organization. The point is that cybercriminals don't have a limit when they target your organization so why should you keep it limited? You should give the contract to the hackers who would be able to execute social-engineering, physical tests, DoS and all the other types of tests at the same time to check how much power the security frameworks of your system has and how much stress it can sustain.

Time to Execute the Ethical Hacking Plan

Ethical hacking demands persistence on the part of the owners of an organization. You need to stay patient while you hand over the security of your firm to an expert ethical hacker. You need to do everything peacefully and quietly to ensure that the process finished smoothly. This is a reconnaissance mission, so you need to harness as much information about your organization as it is possible and then hand it over to the ethical hacker. You need to start with a broad view. Let's see how you should execute your plan.

The very first step is to surf through the internet to find out the online presence of your organization, the computer you are using in the organization, and the network systems along with the IP addresses. Hackers need this information before they execute an attack. They can google the name of your company to see how visible it is in the cyberspace. In addition, they should find them out in other search engines such as Bing.

The next step is to narrow down the scope of the ethical hacking attack by targeting some particular systems that you have been testing. Whether you intend to hit upon the physical systems or any kind of web application, you should run a casual assessment that can help you collect key information about your systems.

Then you can allow the hacker to conduct an ethical hacking test. The most important step of ethical hacking is to ensure that you are efficiently assessing the results of what you have uncovered. You should evaluate the results and form a connection between specific vulnerabilities. That's how you will be able to create a solid defense mechanism that could deter any attack on exploiting these vulnerabilities. At the end of an ethical hacking test, you will have plenty of information about the systems of your company. You will know how these systems are working, what are the weaknesses that a cybercriminal can exploit and what are the remedies. You will feel more confident about doing business than you have felt ever before. (Beaver, 2004)

Chapter 8

The Internet of Things
and Vulnerability

The Internet of things is more crucial for businesses than ever before. They are developing fast on the back of cutting-edge innovations but the security aspect is hardly a priority for most of the innovators and creators. There is often little to no built-in security for the systems. Home users buy and use certain smart technologies without bothering to care about the number of dangers these technologies can bring with them. Security questions have really dogged certain internet of things (IoT) since the day they were invented for people to use. Almost everyone ranging from vendors to domestic consumers are concerned more than ever that the devices they are using may be compromised sooner or later. The real problem is worse than that. Vulnerable internet of things devices can be hacked into, exposing the user to fraud and data breach. Hackers nowadays tend to threaten even some pretty highly secure devices.

Still, there is hardly any debate on what the origin of the problem is. Does the problem pertain to the building phase of the device, or the deployment phase, or the management phase of the IoT systems? In addition, it remains to be seen what can be done for mitigation of the issues? This chapter discusses the weaknesses of the internet of things and solutions to eliminate these weaknesses.

An Overview of the Weaknesses of the Internet of Things

The internet of things is weak, has guessable and easy to break passwords. Some of the threats to the internet of things (IoT) have unique nature while others target the ecosystem of the application. Each threat, in any case, leads to the loss of privacy, recruitment of devices or loss of control. Basically, the internet of things (IoT) makes use of the internet connectivity that has embedded technology that allows them to be under control from a remote location. As there was no security planned for these devices, the level of security breaches is touching the skies, generating headlines across the world. People are so careless about IoT devices that they don't take it seriously to set hard-to-guess passwords that are pretty lengthy and include numbers and symbols. Proper risk assessment and security are crucial for your company and your home devices.

Internet of things (IoT) devices can range from vehicles and home appliances to electronics and actuators that allow these things to get connected. There has been news about a cyberattack on a casino. Cybercriminals, as it was reported, used an underwater thermostat, connected to the internet, to hack into the casino. Through the security breach, the attackers got access through the back doors of the casino and broke into the gambler database. It was creepy and chilling for most businesses. Who would imagine that a thermostat would be used to sneak into the cyberspace and steal precious data? Without a doubt, it sent shivers up the spines of most businessmen.

These devices are making their way into commercial businesses as well as at homes. One of the highly popular devices is Google's Alexa. Some other popular devices are Smart door locks, Google Home and Smart hubs. Other devices include thermostats, internet cameras, irrigation controllers and smart vents.

One of the most common vulnerabilities in these IoT devices is that they are pretty vulnerable to ransomware attacks. We have already discussed the adverse effects of this ransomware that affected people in over 150 countries of the world. The notorious cyberattack had affected around 55 traffic cameras in Australia and Virginia. It had also disrupted the British National Health Service. This was one of the largest ransomware attacks in the history of cybercrimes, and it continues to remain a high-level threat. This is was not a direct attack on the IoT devices but this really showed how a cyberattack could affect all the devices with a user interface.

Attackers may find out a weak web interface and exploit it. They may use weak credentials to access the interface and steal data, initiate a denial of service attack, and can also take over control of your device, locking you out. In 2014, cybercriminals used a weak web interface to compromise Asus routers. The only weakness was that they had default usernames and passwords.

If there is insufficient authentication, it can be exploited by cyberattackers. This kind of vulnerability can be easily manipulated to get access to an interface. Attackers can trigger a denial of service attack and compromise the data on the device. Hackers used this technique to get access to the Jeep Cherokee via Wi-Fi-connectivity. The weakness was that the Wi-Fi password for the Jeeps was generated on the basis of the time when the car was started. If the hacker can easily guess the time, they can use some brute force methods to get access to the head unit of the jeep.

Sometimes attackers use weak network services to attack the device. These compromised devices can be used as a facilitator or medium to attack other devices. Transport encryption is another problem that is exploited by hackers. This welcomes 3rd parties to view the data that is traveling between networks. They can see what has been traveling and steal at will This is the easiest vulnerability to be exploited.

Is There a Remedy?

You should not give data to the internet of things (IoT) that don't need it. This is the foremost security tip to keep in mind if you want to keep your (IoT) secure from any kind of cyberattacks. Here is a rundown of the list of the tips that could aid you in saving your company from falling prey to some common mistakes that could disrupt their business. Let's go through a rundown of the methods to minimize the cybersecurity threats.

- You should update every password on all the devices in your home or office. You should take the utmost care in using a device that has default passwords. In addition, you should set minimum permissions that would be needed to allow the devices to function properly.

- You must stay ready to do your homework about everything that goes on the network. You should also be ready to keep in view all the back-end and cloud services that are working inside your network. For example, some people use Google docs to store their data and some businesses set up their remote offices at an online platform such as slack and basecamp. Before you take the step to switch your workspace or share your personal information at online platforms, you should conduct considerable research on what is the security situation of the company you are working with and how secure is the online space that you have been using.

- It is always a good idea to create a separate network for your workspace of work data to avoid any attempt of penetration.

You can set up your workspace inside the bounds of a firewall and under careful watch when it comes to the security of the IoT devices. This can really help keep the insecure devices away from the key resources and networks. This is a kind of proactive approach to make your business perfectly secure.

- Another tip that you must follow is never using the features that you are not going to need. For example, you should keep the microphones of your smart TV off if you don't need them. Just display of the TV should suffice your needs. You always have an open option for deactivating the microphone and also its internet connection. This will make your IoT device safe and secure. There was a famous episode of smart TV hacking in the United States of America. Wikileaks contained some files that indicated that CIA agents used a smart tv malware named Weeping Angel to spy on people. Weeping Angel was an app that ran in the background switching on the microphone of the smart tv and recording the audio. The app was so powerful that it could manipulate the Wi-Fi that the smart tv was using and recover its keys. It also could access the usernames and passwords that are stored on the tv browser. Another feature of the app allowed operators to record the audio even when the tv was shut down. (Browster, 2017)

- Another important tip to maximize the security of your IoT device is to look out for any kind of physical compromise that could put your data and identity at risk. The devices that have a hardware "factory reset" switch that could wipe out any passwords and set the device to default passwords is considered as highly vulnerable. Once I was at the office at my desk when a colleague approached me and demanded that I looked into his mobile device that was locked by mistake. The user no longer remembered the password. I had some working knowledge of how to switch on the mobile device in the setup mode. So I switched it off and pressed a couple of keys simultaneously to switch it back on in the setup mode. I used the volume keys to scroll up and down to click on several options to reach the right one that could allow me to reset the password. I was taking guidance from a YouTube video that was running on my own mobile phone. It tool around five minutes before I reached the factory reset option. It was a hard reset that wiped out all the passwords on the device and gave it a restart. The phone restarted soon after the reset finished. It was perfectly unlocked. It was a moderately priced smartphone that most people use. I was wondering if my phone remains in the hands of a skillful person, what havoc he could wreak on my life? I have lots of things running on my phone. There is a complete detail of my bank account. He could transfer all the money to his own account without my authorization. He also could disrupt my virtual workspaces because I use Slack and Basecamp to do my work. That's wasn't really reassuring. I was scared by the lack of security on that smartphone device. So you need to check it before you buy it. If there is any kind of factory reset option, you should avoid buying that device.

- If you are unable to block the incoming traffic to the IoT device you are using, you should make sure that you don't leave open any software ports that someone could use for gaining control.

- Do some encryption on things. You should encrypt any kind of data you are sending or receiving through your IoT device. Do it regularly to keep the data secure. Most of the data is lost because we have not encrypted it. Hackers can interrupt it midway in the air and steal the packets, and you won't know a single thing about it.

- You should adopt the habit of doing regular updates to the software and operating systems of your IoT device. Some devices update on their own whenever they get connected to a reliable internet connection. On top of that, you should manually check for the updates on the IoT devices and make sure that they are getting patches. The best advice is to avoid the equipment that doesn't update regularly.

- Sometimes manufacturers stop supporting different devices and software. For example, Microsoft stopped supporting the Microsoft cell phone devices that they had launched earlier on. Similarly, Microsoft has stopped supporting the Windows 7 operating system which means that users are not getting any updates for their security definitions that are crucial to ensure the security of the device. If a manufacturer has stopped supporting a device, it means the device is now vulnerable to cyberattackers and you should not purchase it.

Chapter 9

Vulnerabilities in Critical Infrastructures

Critical infrastructure is the assets, systems and networks that play a crucial role in the security of the nation-state. If they fail to remain operational, the security of the reason may be compromised and its economy slips into chaos. It also has a really bad impact on the public health and safety of the region. Critical infrastructure is generally similar in almost all the nation-states of the world because it deals with some basic needs of life. There is a slight difference in different countries in the division of critical infrastructure.

I'll explain the critical infrastructure of the United States for reference. 16 critical infrastructure sectors are considered as vital to the United States and which, if destroyed or incapacitated in the wake of a cyberattack, can land the country into serious trouble. These critical infrastructure sectors include the chemical sector, the commercial facilities sector, the manufacturing sector, the communications sector, the dams sector, the defense industrial base sector etc. Almost for all the other nations, these sectors remain the same only with a little deviation.

An Overview of the Threats Faced by the Critical Infrastructure

There are concerns among different government circles that critical infrastructure is at risk of a cyberattack. The concerns for a sophisticated cyberattack on the critical infrastructure has its roots in the services this infrastructure offer to the citizens of a country. Minor disruption to the services can bring the government on its knees because of the mega interruption in the flow of public administration and the chaos attached to it in the form of public protests. For example, if the water department of the nation is subjected to a sophisticated cyberattack, the chances are high that a huge number of people will be affected in a country. Water, being a basic need of humans, will adversely affect the public peace. Soon, people will come to take to the streets and there will be chaos everywhere if the services are not brought back to normal in a short span of time.

Cybersecurity has shifted its course from being a money-driven thing to becoming a major force in shaping up the international relations among different countries. Nowadays, cybercriminals lookout for certain vulnerabilities in the critical infrastructure of a nation to gain access to some useful and highly classified information. Once they grab hold of an important piece of information, they are able to take over the entire organization or at a certain activity that the department is running. To make this worse, they can opt to paralyze the system and kill an entire activity that will turn out to be chaotic. (Cybersecurity for Critical Infrastructure, 2019)

Cybersecurity has to rely on a wide range of internal and external factors. All devices that are connected to a network have certain backdoors that can be exploited by hackers who want to gain access to an organization. With the access to the organization, the hackers also succeed in getting access to certain systems that the organization has been connected to. The way cybersecurity breaches have been across organizations of the world, cybersecurity has become a top priority for almost everyone in the setup of critical infrastructure.

The problem is that every device and system is connected to the internet that strengthens it and also makes it weak. There is a very well saying that a cybersecurity framework in critical infrastructure is as powerful as the most fragile of the devices in the setup. Put a weak device in the network and risk a breach. It will help hackers take down the entire organization in a matter of hours. Therefore, the organization must keep in its consideration the weakest of devices in the system and clear away any kind of ambiguity with respect to security. (Cybersecurity for Critical Infrastructure, 2019)

There has been a significant rise in social media usage and internet connectivity across the world. According to an estimate, around 2.5 billion people had been connected to the internet across the world in 2014. The figure now touches around 3 billion. The internet of things is on the rise and as I have alluded to in the past chapters, and they are the most fragile type of devices and they are most time vulnerable to an attack by a malicious hacker.

There is a number of attacks that can happen. The most worrying thing about IP surveillance cams is that hackers might choose to use these cybersecurity attacks to create cracks in different parts of the critical infrastructure they want to target. Through these cracks, they can infiltrate and make it as a hopping point to collect some classified data which they can sell on the dark web or to a broker who would then sell it to a particular state. Another dangerous point of view is that this kind of breach can be utilized to take over a number of controllers in the system. (Cybersecurity for Critical Infrastructure, 2019)

If a cyberattack happens on the oil and gas industry, they can either collect crucial information about the supply of oil or they can stop functioning of rigs or oil well, pushing the oil and gas supply to a halt. This can be catastrophic if the heads of the infrastructure and the agencies of the country are not anticipating the attack. Once again, the example of Ukraine from the past chapters is another glaring incident to explain how a critical infrastructure can be attacked and how lethal the attack can be in terms of the level of destruction attached to it. A shut-down power grid produces a trickle-down effect on the entire administration of the country that has come under severe attack. When the power sector shuts down, it triggers the industrial sector to close operations. The industrial sector may include some strategic industries such as the weaponry and export industry that runs the revenue of the country. When a stopper has been inserted into the mouth of the industrial sector, it will take its toll on the public in the form of loss of employment and a rapid rise in the prices of daily use things. Power sector's shutting down will also compel the telecom sector and broadband companies to shut down operations after a while unless there is enough fuel in the generators that keep the cell phone towers running in the absence of power. (Cybersecurity for Critical Infrastructure, 2019)

The Repercussions of Not Caring for Cybersecurity

The energy and power sectors among all the critical infrastructure sectors, are dubbed as the most important sectors because they are prone to cyberattacks. Hackers view these sectors as engines to run the other sectors. If they go down, with them, go down all the other key critical infrastructure departments. Transportation will be severely affected if trains don't revive power. Shutting down the power sector also adversely affects the water and agriculture sector.

The states must adopt key measures to harden the entire system against cyberattacks but it should specifically pay attention to power and energy sectors that are of strategic importance. Just imagine if a hostile country attacks your country by bringing down the power sector. Your houses will be dark and there will be no cable service that means there will be no news. As a head of the state, you will lose half the war just because you will be unable to communicate with the public that means that the turbulence levels in the country will be an all-time high. This is enough to push the country out of control. A malfunction in the cybersecurity realm in critical infrastructure can cause catastrophic failures that would put to a strategic disadvantage in a state of war. If you want to imagine what would happen in the absence of power due to a cybersecurity attack, you should keep in view what happens when a storm knocks down the power grids. At least we know that the storm is responsible for the chaos we have been suffering from. In the wake of a cybersecurity attack, the element of fear also takes its toll on the public. (Cybersecurity for Critical Infrastructure, 2019)

What Should Be the Steps to Protect These Sites?

Of course, the markets are full of tools that you should use in the wake of an attack, but equally important is the fact that you should not forget about applying some important standards on your systems. Organizations need to draft policies that ensure that you are following the best safety practices for your organization. The best practices must affect the selection as well as the configuration of the certain devices that are used in the environments. As the head of a state, you should not only draft policies and bring them in black and white, but also apply them to mitigate the risk factor in the system. (Cybersecurity for Critical Infrastructure, 2019)

There should be adopted a standard cybersecurity site plan just like a security site plan (SSP) that tackles the physical security of an organization. Some public officials harbor the opinion that they can cover up the cybersecurity in its entirety just like they do with the physical security, but they fail to realize the fact that physical security spans around the boundaries of infrastructure such as a power plant. You know the spread of the walls and you also know the gates. You have the option to install a razor wire around the facility to maximize security. You can go for passing an electric current through the fences to deter intruders. There will be CCTV cameras and a force of guards to insulate the facility, and also there will be a sophisticated security alarm system that would start screaming as soon as it detects the slightest of suspicious movement around the facility. When it comes to cybersecurity, things get all the more different. Hackers want to sneak into the system with as little noise as possible.

Moreover, there is no limit to the range of attacks. A hacker can reside in a tiny city of Africa while he targets a corporation in the United States. Hackers are always seeking ways to find the loopholes that they can exploit to inflict maximum loss on the company. The difficulty in maintaining cybersecurity lies in the fact that you have to stay on top of the situation all the time. It is always better to anticipate an attack and to prevent it rather than being a victim of an attack and then dealing with it.

Once a malware hits the system, it takes some time to be traced out and more time to eliminate from the system. You have to make a clear assessment of the processes of cybersecurity and you need to map out the vulnerabilities that exist in your system. These two steps are just the same as in the creation of an SSP. You have to be diligent in maintaining the changes, and also keeping your cyber team up to date with the latest knowledge and tools to deal with the latest cyberattacks. If the hacker is not limiting himself to old methods, why should you? And if you would try to put a limit on you, you will regret it because the cybercriminal will be way ahead of you by the time you realize his presence in the system. Does this sound creepy and scary? (Cybersecurity for Critical Infrastructure, 2019)

The problem is that a single weak spot in the system is enough for a determined hacker to enter the system and corrupt it before you know what happened. You need to look for the products that you can easily fit into your organization's security plan. One key solution to combat cybersecurity breaches is to team up with partners that have a good reputation, and that follow the best practices available in the market. In addition, the security firm you are teaming up with should be open and transparent in its dealings. You should be intimated about the nature of the threats your organization is facing and the solutions that the security firm has been implementing to resolve the issue. (Cybersecurity for Critical Infrastructure, 2019)

There is a possibility that a potential fallout of a network breach happens inside a critical infrastructure sector turns destructive; its effects can be felt across a huge number of critical sectors. When you are taking steps for securing devices inside your organization, one of the top factors is to acquire equipment from different companies that have been committed to deliver the best practices for ensuring security in the organization. They must show you the track record of doing so in the end.

There is a key factor that organizations must not ignore if they want to ensure the security of the organization in the cyber realm, and that is ensuring end-to-end cybersecurity for all the interconnected devices and the systems available at a facility. To achieve this goal, you can pair up with like-minded organizations that would offer complimentary tech and are highly committed to making the products secure. (Cybersecurity for Critical Infrastructure, 2019)

The third most important factor for securing the network systems and the devices is ensuring the implementation and enforcement of robust security policies through the facility. There should be standard procedures in place to minimize the possibility of a human error that would undermine the cybersecurity of the entire facility.

You should also install certain device management tools that can make things easier for you to ensure that all the devices are properly configured in accordance with the best practices. Foolproof cybersecurity focuses on the assessment of risks as well as taking proper steps to combat the glaring cyberattacks. Cybersecurity can only work if you are willing to work with the right lot of people and also willing to implement the best policies. If you can keep all these factors in mind, you can be able to beef up cybersecurity in your organization for better protection of your critical infrastructure sites and the assets. (Cybersecurity for Critical Infrastructure, 2019)

Chapter 10

Economic Impact of Cybersecurity

It is critical that we must calculate the economic cost of cybersecurity before we move on to introduce it in our organizations. The assessment should be correct and you should also have a categorical estimate of the cost of cybersecurity for different sectors of your organization. Not only for the defense of the different sectors of an organization but also for the prevention of cyberattacks in the future. More than ever, we need our assets and intellectual property to be fully protected in the wake of cyberattacks. Policymakers of a country or of an organization must take into account the scope of the cybercrime when they are drafting security policies. The policies must include the expenditures on the execution of these policies.

This chapter will shed light on different aspects of expenditures when it comes to cybersecurity. It should be a part of the budget-making process to estimate how much funds go into securing cyberspace around an organization. The estimates ought to be as much realistic as they can be. The nature of cybercrimes has considerably changed and that's why the amount of financial resources that were earlier on injected into the systems to keep them running needs to be modified as per the latest requirements. In the start of the cybercrimes, it was restricted to loot money from a bank or a financial institution or extortion. Now cybercrime has been transformed into something big. It has been converted into cyber-espionage and cyber warfare that has taken the world by storm. These new challenges have added a new dimension to the world of cybersecurity. This brings us to a higher amount of funds that must go into defending the organization against these threats.

Nowadays, there are different aspects of cybersecurity, such as the municipal level, at the state level and at the federal level. Each corporate sector and even retail businesses have to invest in cybersecurity to protect themselves. Sometimes, a scientific study must be conducted to assess the level of risks that loom over an organization. At other times, a forensic security audit needs to be conducted by cybersecurity experts to point out weaknesses and possible loopholes that can become potential gateways for cyberattackers. Apart from that, if you have to run a thorough ethical hacking plan to make an accurate risk assessment in your organization.

I was once hired by a finance consultancy firm to initiate an ethical hacking plan after the firm suffered from a heavy loss because of a mega data breach. I had to charge them thousands of dollars because of the amount of time, energy, and the number of equipment I had to put into the ethical hacking plan. It was overwhelming at times because I had to go through trash cans, the dustbins, the database, the storeroom, the servers and all possible loopholes that could be exploited. I had to double up the fees because I had accepted the responsibility to prepare a report on the reasons behind the first attack and the estimates of the loss. This increased the amount of work and the time that would be spent on the process. If you make it a habit to run a thorough ethical hacking test once a year, you can minimize the cost of cybersecurity because you won't have to pay for the preparation of the report of the past incident, and secondly, there won't be any incident if you remain proactive.

Other different costs can come into play when we are protecting the cyberspace in an organization. You will have to spend money on antivirus software, intrusion prevention software, and other such things. You will have to purchase a number of security devices and networking software that could prevent any attempt of infiltration at the global level. You will have to include certain managers, executives and information technology security officers.

Still, the cost of cybersecurity is a bit complicated as it is pretty tough to sum up the reporting costs and the real financial losses in the system. The real financial losses are pretty hard to estimate because the total cost of a loss of intellectual property can be pretty tough to estimate. In the past, there have been cases in which businesses had to file for bankruptcy and also had to shut down their businesses due to the loss of intellectual property. Another cost factor materializes in terms of loss of reputation because that drives away existing customers and also potential prospects for future business. Even the cost accounting of the loss you have suffered from because of the cyberattack.

Cybersecurity breaches that target a nation's strategic assets such as its military programs and governmental agencies, add to the cost factors of a cyberattack. Another cost factor is securing the defense of the nation in terms of cybersecurity. Cyber-espionage is on the rise as we have witnessed in a wide range of case studies in the past chapters. Countries have to set aside a considerable amount of sum to deter any attempt of espionage on their strategic facilities. This has turned out to be an additional burden on national exchequers.

How you can measure the economic impact of a possible cyberattack has gained lots of importance as more and more business leaders have shown interest in beefing up their cybersecurity networks. Business adversaries are getting more competitive in their respective fields and they are seeking an edge over others no matter how they get this advantage. Breaking into the databases and computer systems of adversary companies is a way to operate profitably in the eyes of some business owners, which is without a doubt below the belt. This quest to gain greater knowledge about the business strategies of their adversaries have compelled certain business owners to create a foolproof strategy to tackle cyberattacks. This demands a dedicated allocation of the budget at the start of the financial year. Different analysts have approached this issue in their own style. They have been using the impact model types which are speculative in their conclusions and assumptions.

Chapter 11

Solutions to the
Problem of Cybersecurity

The greatest challenge of the modern world is to secure cyberspace, of which you are a continuous inhabitant. We spend more time in the cyber world than in the real world, but still, we hardly do anything to secure it. It is the greatest challenge to solve the Cybersecurity problems that we face nowadays because of the enormity of the problem. The security fundamentals require some insight into the control measures to safeguard the confidentiality and integrity of the data of a business. In the absence of strict controls, cyberattackers may go on to threaten to bring down entire systems and expose sensitive data or right away shut down the entire systems of a business. These types of attacks can lead to some pretty grave business losses.

Cybercriminals can break into the firewalls and access control centers to penetrate into a network and inflict some serious damage. If you want to neutralize this rising threat, you need to train your employees in the field of cybersecurity and install some aggressive controls to protect sensitive information. Anyone who wants to learn about the cybersecurity fundamentals should learn expert management techniques to maintain the confidentiality of business information.

Cyberattackers have not adopted the latest practices to boost up the efficiency of their attacks. Some of them have transformed their skills into enterprise skills and they are not only selling but also licensing hacking tools to the aspirants of the field. This has become a thriving business for a few experts. The sale of zero-day technology is a brilliant example of technology that is being sold in the open market where it is being commoditized. Even ransomware has become a service.

There has been a full ecosystem in place for cybercriminals to leverage their activities. They can use tremendous resources from that eco-system to make the attack more severe and lethal.

Solutions to Cybersecurity Issues

Cybersecurity issues don't have a single solution for all kinds of attacks. A multi-pronged approach can turn out to be the best solution in all cases. Solutions must include sophisticated technology and human components such as training of the employees and spreading awareness among the board members.

The very first approach is the real-time intelligence approach that would prevent and also contain active cyberattacks. You have by now realized the fact that cyber-attacks get more costly if there is a delay in identifying the nature and the core of the attack. There are multiple ways to protect yourself from a cybersecurity threat.

The very first technique is to form a multi-layered defense strategy. You should ensure that the strategy must cover the enterprise in its entirety, and all the endpoints, mobile devices, and applications should be well-protected. It is always a better approach to install a two or three-factor authentication to make the data on the systems accessible to the users. The same authentication process should be installed to access the network.

There should be a third-party vendor assessment for the cybersecurity system. You should implement the least-privilege policy in the organization that means no one has a special privilege to access sensitive information in your systems. You should develop it into a long-standing habit to review the application of credentials when it comes to any third-party application or software. You can take a step further to place in a service level agreement (SLA) that obligates the 3rd party vendors to comply with the security policies of your company. If you have already signed the agreement, you have the right to review if the 3rd party has been complying with your security policy.

One important thing that we miss out on is to back up the data that has been generating each single day in our offices. It is good to have faith in your security systems, but it is better to back up your data by the time you are moving toward the wrap up of the office hours. That's who you can save a lot of money that would be spent in case your data is stolen and removed from your systems. In addition, you will be perfectly safe from ransomware attacks.

Don't be afraid of patching frequently. A software patch is a kind of snippet of code update that is installed in existing software. More often, these patches are temporary fixes when the software is in update mode and has yet to hit the markets. A patch is normally used to fix a bug in the software or address the latest security vulnerability. It can also go on to install new drivers on your system.

IT problems are not normal business problems as they are concerned with the employees as much as it is concerned with the technical department. A cybersecurity breach can be really frustrating because the enemy is hidden. Most of the businesses around the world still consider it as something that is not a business issue, but they are far from the truth. The truth is that each business must have a cyber threat management team that would train the employees by laying foundation of a cyber risk awareness culture in your organization.

Also, it is recommended that certain organizations must designate their chief information security officer. The employees must be trained to know what the signs of a cybersecurity breach are so that when one happens, they are ready to detect it and report it to the head of the security branch. In addition, the employees must be trained to open emails in the right way and also they should know how to respond to a takeover attempt by malicious hackers.

The top solution to tackle cybersecurity issues is to pick up the right company that offers the best strategy to suit your business needs. You need a seasoned security service provider that is capable of delivering an adaptable solution in an effective way and also offers a seamless solution.

You should get hold of top-class antivirus software that can safeguard your computer systems from any kind of attack. An efficient antivirus program can scan your computer systems, the emails that you and your staff receive and watch the browsing done during office hours. If the antivirus software detects any threat, it can remove it right away before it can infect your computer systems. Don't forget to update the antivirus software right after the company releases a new version of definitions. This will help you deal with the latest errors that are present in the online realm. Most of the antivirus programs include a kind of automatic download feature when the computer system gets connected to a valid internet connection. Some employees are prone to turn off the antivirus program to boost up the speed of the computer system that is not a good exercise. The antivirus program must keep running all the time to maximize security. Only in this way you can ensure that your system is being continuously scanned for viruses and preventing any potential threat.

What If You Have Already Been Attacked?

The solutions are different in case your computer systems have already suffered from a cyberattack. If you suspect that any dubious file has been download on the system, your first step should be to delete the file from the system and save your computer. Don't try to open it before deleting it. A single click can cost you your privacy. After you have deleted the file, you should run an immediate security scan to detect if there are any effects left of the suspicious file or not. If your team detects a key-logger on the computer system, you should immediately direct them to reset all the passwords on your computer systems for all the linked accounts to that system.

If you are running a business, you need to have a central administration capability on the local as well as cloud server, that's how you can store files and folders on a single server that is accessible to a bunch of officials. As a business, you should make sure that you have access to a cloud server for storing important data. That's how you can save yourself from extreme loss in the wake of a cyberattack.

You need to make cybersecurity perfect by determining which resources you need for better protection. You should be ready to identify the threats to your business and the risks involved in your day-to-day transactions. You should be proactive in calculating the precautionary measures that are needed to address the threats and to secure the assets of your business. You should be ready to manage certain security breaches. You should keep updating the protection measures if it is necessary.

Chapter 12

Future Trends in Cybersecurity

Cybersecurity has been a hot topic for organizations and businesses across the world. Every company has its own priorities as well as insights to follow. Some of the current trends in the cybersecurity realm are about the types of attacks that are shaping up in the industry, different methods of preventing the attack and the types of industries that are on the target list. Other trends in the cybersecurity realm that are currently at the forefront are related to the methods and technologies that are being used to defend against a cyberattack. These trends include a sizable reduction in security vulnerabilities as individuals and the corporate sector are now more aware of the security vulnerabilities in their computer systems. Networks are getting more secure and better at dealing with cyber threats. Data privacy remains on the rise which has made data more secure. In addition, the collection, as well as analysis of data, are more efficient as compared to past practices.

There have been some top security trends in the IT industry that have dominated it until now. Multi-factor authentication is on the top of the list. It has considerably secured the cyberspace. I have set up a two-factor verification system for my Gmail accounts and it is working quite well in securing my email account from any kind of attack. This has made passwords more secure than ever. In addition to this trend, retinal scans and biometrics systems are also on the rise. (The Top Cybersecurity Trends in 2019 (and What to Expect in 2020), 2019)

An Overview of the Current Trends in the Cybersecurity Realm

It should not come as a surprise that phishing remained at the top of the list in the cybersecurity trends, but it has changed its form a little bit as it is now not just about emails alone though emails remained a popular threat vector. Cybercriminals have also adopted other vectors to reach out to potential victims and to trick them into performing a certain action such a yielding information, login credentials, and extortion. Nowadays, phishing also involves SMS texting attacks that are now being dubbed as smishing. Smishing encompasses everything from communications via LinkedIn and other social media platforms to telephone calls. These kind of attacks are getting more rampant by which the person the call demands from you your ID number, account number or any other sensitive information. (The Top Cybersecurity Trends in 2019 (and What to Expect in 2020), 2019)

Use of mobile phones as an attack vector was also on the rise. Hackers shifted their focus from other vectors to mobile phones keeping in view the rise in the use of mobile phones. Almost everyone has a cell phone that he or she carries wherever they go. Well, mobile phones were earlier on used for calling and messaging to your loved ones and office colleagues, but since the rise of smartphones, phone calls, and messaging is just the thing of the past. They are now being used for more advanced services such as operating a bank account through a mobile application. You can send or receive payment, pay utility bills, pay for mobile top-up and also transfer any amount of cash to a friend or a business partner. You can also pay the school fee of your kid. Now air flights are being booked from mobile phones and hotel rooms are being rented by just a single click. In fact, for every important task of life, we have an application to download and play. You can download a game app if you are bored and a yoga app if you want to do some exercise. You can download a book set to read your favorite book and there is just no shortage of things that you can do on a cell phone. (The Top Cybersecurity Trends in 2019 (and What to Expect in 2020), 2019)

The point is that the convenience made available by mobile phones is so vast that it is difficult to grasp it in a single paragraph, but this convenience has not arrived without its risks for the end-users. Cybercriminals can hack into a mobile phone and inflict considerable loss on the user by making unauthorized transactions or making a fake call or message that could result in loss of money.

Another visible trend in the cybersecurity realm is the rise of ransomware. Cybercriminals have been attacking individuals and enterprises to extort a heavy amount of cash in return for unlocking their databases. I have already discussed this topic in its entirety in the past chapters.

One of the most important cybersecurity trends is the increase in emphasis on the privacy of data, compliance, and sovereignty. States and industries across the globe have begun taking some critical looks at the current state of their data. They are reviewing their privacy policies. Data sovereignty has different forms. Corporations are now being regulated by governments all around the world to adopt standard practices with respect to data that they collect from their users. One prominent example is the issue of Facebook and Cambridge Analytica. (The Top Cybersecurity Trends in 2019 (and What to Expect in 2020), 2019)

A whistleblower described how a firm that was linked to the former Trump adviser, namely Steve Bannon compiled user data to target US voters during the presidential elections. The data firm namely Cambridge Analytica, worked with the election team of Donald Trump and had earlier on worked with the Brexit campaign had taken the job to harvest data from millions of Facebook profiles mostly of US voters. The story revealed the biggest data breach in the history of cybersecurity. They used the data to develop a robust and advanced software program to predict as well as influence voters who were about to cast their votes in the near future to vote in a new president. (The Top Cybersecurity Trends in 2019 (and What to Expect in 2020), 2019)

The whistleblower revealed that the company acted on the will of Steve Bannon, one of the key advisors for President Donald Trump. They used the information harvested from Facebook without authorization to build up a system that could target individual voters by tailoring personalized advertisements.

The data was harvested through an application named as thisisyourdigitallife. During the time of data harvesting, hundreds of users were paid for the survey they had to take. It was a kind of personality test. The participants were told that their data would be used for academic purposes only but in reality, it was used in the election campaign. The application exceeded its mandate and went on to collect the data of the Facebook friends of the participants of the test. This enabled the handlers to harvest tens of millions of accounts. Facebook allowed the harvest but banned to use the data for selling or advertising purposes, but the damage was done and the role of Facebook in this saga of events came into the limelight. Questions were raised on the role of Facebook in shaping up the results of the presidential election in the United States. Both Cambridge Analytica and Facebook became the focus of the news. Politicians dubbed it as an attempt of political targeting with the help of the humongous amount of data that was harvested illegally. (The Top Cybersecurity Trends in 2019 (and What to Expect in 2020), 2019)

The Chief Executive Officer of Facebook Mark Zuckerberg was summoned by the US Congress to answer on the role of Facebook in the data harvest. Lots of other questions were raised, such as how secure a user is while he is using the services of a social media platform and how transparent the privacy policy of Facebook is when it comes to users' information and its security.

In the wake of this kind of attack, different types of legislations were made and political leaders and human rights activists across the globe strove to compel governments to legislate on the matter. All agreed that individuals should be informed about how their information is being used or will be used. It has also been agreed that individuals should know how to disallow their information to be shared with a third-party. Data security and sovereignty were increased. Also, there had been an increase in the security of personal information by using encryption as well as other kinds of mechanisms. (The Top Cybersecurity Trends in 2019 (and What to Expect in 2020), 2019)

Another trend that topped the list was the rise in investments in the field of cyber automation that is a very important advantage in the field of cybersecurity. It has succeeded in gaining a kind of foothold in the industry of cybersecurity. On the back of automation, users can easily collect data about certain components of an information system. The data can be used afterward for monitoring purposes. Automated cybersecurity system helps business owners in keeping track of the software and the hardware they have installed in their facilities to watch any kind of suspicious activity. In addition to this, it keeps a record of all the virtual and physical assets well-maintained by keeping them up to date. It can perform certain vulnerability tests to pinpoint different types of vulnerabilities in the system. (The Top Cybersecurity Trends in 2019 (and What to Expect in 2020), 2019)

The Future Trends in Cybersecurity

The future trends among the cybersecurity threats include the rise in the use of Artificial Intelligence technologies by cybersecurity agencies as well as by cybercriminals. Attackers can manipulate AI and generate adversarial systems that harbor two networks to compete for learning a data set. In their quest to learn faster than the other, these adversarial systems would resolve the AI algorithms that are used to secure virtual space. Once they have uncovered an algorithm, they can build their own model to bypass the existing one. Data can be used to train the new model. Machine learning that is a sub-field of Artificial Intelligence is being used to create a lot more convincing as well as personalized messages in phishing attacks that make it easier to steal credentials. It also will make it easier to plant malware in a certain network system.

Crypto-jacking is another technique that is getting common in a fast way. It has become more valuable and is being quite famous in the world of cybercriminals. It is considered as a speedier way to make profits because it is the only technique that can be executed under the radars of a security system.

Cybercrime has developed into the greatest threat that corporations and governments face across the world. There has been a considerable rise in the number of attacks on public and private computer systems. Cyberattacks are becoming the fastest growing crimes in the United States, and they are increasing the operational cost of business across the world. The most troublesome fact is that these attacks are getting more sophisticated with the passage of each day.

The past few years had been interesting with respect to cybersecurity on the back of considerable developments in the nature of the strength of cyberattacks and also in the countermeasures. The way this field is making progress across the world, the years ahead are going to be quite interesting. The past few years have seen a significant rise in the number of cyberattacks and also in the intensity of the attacks. That troubled a lot of people and also gave way to some viable solutions to counter these problems. Let's take a look at some predictions by experts on the future trends of cybersecurity.

1. The very first trend will be data theft that will be turned into the manipulation of data. Hackers may be seen as manipulators rather than robbers. This type of attack will be different from data theft because it will aim at long-term harm. These attacks will considerably affect the reputation of an organization or an individual or a group of people. It will have the power to make people question the integrity of the data they have been using. Big corporations have initiated pilot programs to deploy AI systems for checking the integrity of the data in their systems. Machine learning and AI combined will go on to reinvent the world of cybersecurity. This can happen on the back of the enormous benefits offered by AI. Some of them are stated as under:

- AI-based cybersecurity solutions are ready to work round the clock without taking a toll on your hot purse.

- AI-based cybersecurity solutions can respond in as minimum a time as a millisecond as compared to the traditional response to the cyberattack that takes hours, if not days, to topple up the attacker.

- AI-based cybersecurity solutions aim at simplification of the process of collection of data and its analysis.

- AI-based cybersecurity solutions can be paired up into each other to boost up the response to an enhanced threat and any kind of suspicious activity through predictive analytics.

- AI-based cybersecurity solutions offer you greater access to some valuable amount of data that helps the cybersecurity professionals improve their performance and decision-making capability.

- AI-based cybersecurity solutions are aiding each other in the creation of better as well as an accurate biometric-based login procedure.

On the one hand, AI will help improve the cybersecurity while on the other hand, it will also help the attackers. Let's see how attackers will set a new trend by using AI to achieve their objectives. Let's break down the cons of using Artificial Intelligence.

1. The attackers will use AI-based cyber technologies as they offer speed and efficiency.

   AI-based cybersecurity solutions can turn out to be pretty expensive than the traditional approaches.

   AI-based cybersecurity solutions need more training for cybersecurity professionals to make them effective and easy to operate.

2. There will be a boom in the job market for cybersecurity experts. Analysts believe that the world will witness a shortage of cybersecurity experts in the days to arrive because of the high demand by big and small organizations. It will be the attacks on the workplace that will compel organizations to hire cybersecurity experts on a permanent

basis. Companies will gradually realize either by experience or by the theory that an effective and tangible cybersecurity policy demanded that a permanent position should be created in the organization. In the same way, companies will stress on the need for internal training of employees. Rather than opting for generic cybersecurity programs, companies will tailor the training programs to fulfill their specific needs.

3. The third trend that is going to make waves in the realm of cybersecurity is the production of the Internet of Things (IoT) that is secure by design. This trend is likely to gain steam by the year 2021 or later because at the moment, the masses have not realized the inherent weakness in the designs of IoT devices. This is going to take some time before the world sees the weaknesses in these devices that hackers can exploit. As the IoT devices will rise in devices, they will create problems for individuals and organizations and get themselves exposed before the world. It is highly likely that from then on, the production of more secure designs starts across the world. One weakness that I want to be instantly removed is the hard factory reset that allow any person to take control of the device.

4. One trend that is also rampant in the current times will keep going in the future is that attackers will find a soft target in consumers. They will make use of ransomware to target individuals and corporations of all forms, as well as magnitudes. I have already cited the example of the WannaCry attack that held hostage the National Health Service of the United Kingdom in addition to the other organizations around the world. After 2020 and onwards, attacks on consumers will see a significant rise in frequency and magnitude. They will be able to target domestic users

through IoTs such as toys for kids. This field of attack is likely to flourish because small companies are likely to jump in the arena by producing cheap IoT devices that have little to no security. As long as people will keep falling for these cheap devices, there will be insecurity in the world and attackers will keep seeing a heyday. Smart tv is another device that will remain on the hit list of the attackers. The only way to deter such attacks is to purchase the devices that are safe by design. Another way is to sensitize people on the issue of cybersecurity breach. For example, they should be taught to keep the smart TV's mic deactivated.

5. Hackers enjoy immense power because they are anonymous. They commit a crime without leaving a trace behind. The future trends indicate that hackers will be defter at turning themselves invisible and well organized. The power to elude justice and punishment is going to make them more commercialized. They will perhaps establish their own call centers to communicate with the victims. These hackers will likely base themselves in the countries in which cybercrimes are barely regarded as a major crime, or it can be any place where they are out of bounds of the victims.

6. Another important trend that will continue into the future from the present is that spending on cybersecurity will see a considerable increase.

7. Another important trend to watch out for is a continuing streak of attacks on public infrastructure. Cybersecurity attacks in the coming future will highly target utilities. Critical infrastructure is likely to grab hold of its position as the number one target of cyberattackers. Attacks on the infrastructure in the future will affect millions of people as

well as governments around the world. Cybersecurity officials will use old worn out technology to wage attacks on critical infrastructure. In some countries, some critical infrastructure is controlled by a bunch of private organizations that usually struggle with the availability of funds and cannot channelize significant resources into the cybersecurity projects to ensure foolproof security.

8. Cyberattackers are likely to get smarter with time. They can write a targeted code that will outsmart the defenders and seriously undermine their capability to counter the attack or stay ahead of it. In fact, it will be attackers that are going to stay ahead of the time. Attackers are also likely to increase their use of the Dark Web that is a small portion of the Deep Web. They will take cover in the dark web and communicate with other cybercriminals to wage a coordinated attack on big targets such as important critical infrastructures.

9. The cybersecurity breaches are going to get harder to beat. Cybercriminals are likely to grow in their malicious activities with the help of using malicious code. For example, they can create and propagate ransomware that is one of a kind and that will offer victims package to decrypt their files for free in return for sending the ransomware package to three or four other users to infect them. That's how they will invigorate their attack.

10. Another kind of insurance will rise in the wake of some big and rising cybersecurity attacks that will be dubbed as cyber insurance. This type of insurance will increasingly become part of an operational strategy that the insurance industry should tailor certain products that are specific to the needs of the client. Cyber insurance will see a rise and will cover loss

of reputation and customers, loss of any future revenue because of any negative media campaign, and destruction of computer networks and systems.

11. The technological world will anticipate the creation of more jobs in the fields of cybersecurity officers.

Conclusion

The United States has complained that Russian hackers had meddled with the 2016 presidential elections. It was a major incident. Russian hackers hacked into Democratic National Committee and published some pretty confidential emails during the 2016 presidential elections in the United States. This episode produced quite a stir in the legislative corridors of the United States. The power and impact of cybersecurity was revisited and the importance of cybersecurity was elevated, and for the first time, cybersecurity was seen through the context of international relations. The incident was not normal as it had the potential to push the two countries into a kind of conflict. The level of the attack was unprecedented in nature not only in the United States but also across the globe. People had started seeing cybersecurity from a different lens. The incident of Sony Pictures started spinning before the eyes of lots of people who responded with mixed sentiments. Some of them showed a bit of surprise, and others showed extreme concern, while a few showed no reaction at all.

The United States had accused a state of cyberattack in the past in the wake of the attack on Sony Picture Entertainment, but the scale and the impact of this attack were unprecedented. It meant that anyone with a computer could change the course of an election of the most powerful country in the world. But for seasoned cybersecurity experts, this development is not news. Since the advent of the internet back in the mid-1990s, the cyberspace has witnessed some pretty amazing growth that filled the pockets of millions of people due to rapid commercialization but also pushed people into the depths of the crisis. Cybersecurity has now climbed up the ladder and has reached the heads of the state who have started seeing the security of the world in a different way. Scholars of international relations see this new discipline as a subfield of security studies with a special focus on the implications of technology for international security. This takes into account its effects on the sovereignty, power and world governance.

Cybersecurity has gained considerable attention for the past few years on the back of the fact that the attacker is usually not known. This creates a lot of confusion and suspicion that are very unhealthy for a peaceful international environment. Large nations sometimes use proxies to wage cyberattacks and afterward label them as rogue to avoid direct confrontation with the power they are dealing with. We have seen this in the North Koran attack on Sony Pictures. North Korea denounced the attack by appreciated their deed as patriotic. Similarly, when the Russian hackers meddled in the US elections, Vladimir Putin, the Russian president, deny any involvement of the state in the attack but added to the tail of his speech that some patriotic minded Russian hackers might have committed that deed. He appeared to have been appreciating what the hackers had done to the country that had a long history of enmity with Russia.

Had Putin claimed the attack, there would have been an all-out war between the two superpowers of the world. Cybersecurity is playing a crucial role in international relations because the threat of nuclear war and the mutual assured destruction as a result of the war have negatively affected the world strategic scenario. Humans, by nature, cannot live without a contest. Physical war is not possible as the threat of nuclear war keeps looming over the participants of the war. We can see this in the subcontinent where India and Pakistan, the two nuclear powers, have made the subcontinent a nuclear flashpoint in the area. Despite the fact that the possibility of a conflict remains high, the idea of a hot war is not usually pursued by the two countries. So if countries must go into a conflict, they choose the cyber realm to fight each other. Cyberwarfare is an advanced mode of cold wars. I have quoted the example of a scenario in which India responded with a hacking attack after the Pulwama attack. Similarly, North Korea attacked Sony Pictures through a cyber-security breach because it didn't have the power to confront the United States and also it had to give a befitting response to Sony Pictures for making the movie that was a spoof of an assassination attempt on Kim John Un.

Cybersecurity issues are becoming more lethal day by day and it remains doubtful that it will help improve international relations. Up till now, it has shown great potential in complicating and destroying international relations.

This book has explained all the necessary details on the subject of cybersecurity. You have learned what the basics of cybersecurity are. You have also learned what the general motivations are behind an act of cybercriminal. I have discussed in detail was social engineering is and how it is used by malicious hackers to infiltrate a facility. Then I moved on to explain cyber terrorism, its types, and its adverse effects on the modern world such as the relations between countries and the general peace of the country.

References

Browster, T. (2017). Here's How The CIA Allegedly Hacked Samsung Smart TVs -- And How To Protect Yourself. Retrieved from https://www.forbes.com/sites/thomasbrewster/2017/03/07/cia-wikileaks-samsung-smart-tv-hack-security/#4ffd6ca4bcd5

Beaver, K. (2004). Hacking For Dummies [PDF]. Retrieved from http://index-of.co.uk/Hacking-Coleccion/81%20-%20Hacking%20For%20Dummies%20%5B-PUNISHER-%5D.pdf

Cybercrime Damages $6 Trillion By 2021. (n.d). Retrieved from https://cybersecurityventures.com/hackerpocalypse-cybercrime-report-2016/

Cyber terrorism. (n.d). Retrieved from https://web.archive.org/web/20030110120948/http://www.ncsl.org/programs/lis/CIP/cyber-terrorism.htm

Cybersecurity: the motivation behind cyber-hacks [Infographic]. (n.d). Retrieved from https://bigdata-madesimple.com/cybersecurity-the-motivation-behind-cyber-hacks-infographic/

Ranger, S. (2017). Defending against cyberwar: How the cybersecurity elite are working to prevent a digital apocalypse. Retrieved from https://www.techrepublic.com/article/defending-against-cyberwar-how-the-cybersecurity-elite-are-working-to-prevent-a-digital-apocalypse/

The Top Cybersecurity Trends in 2019 (and What to Expect in
    2020). (2019). Retrieved
    fromhttps://www.thesslstore.com/blog/the-top-cyber-
    security-trends-in-2019-and-what-to-expect-in-2020/

9 Latest Cyber-Espionage Affairs. (Mar 7). Retrieved
    fromhttps://blog.eccouncil.org/9-latest-cyber-espionage-
    affairs/

Made in the USA
Coppell, TX
20 December 2020